Business Management for the Equine Industry

Sharon Eastwood, Anne-Lise Riis Jensen and Anna Jordon

Dark Horse Business Consultancy, Ltd

Blackwell
Publishing

© 2006 by Blackwell Publishing Ltd

Editorial Offices:
Blackwell Publishing Ltd, 9600 Garsington Road, Oxford OX4 2DQ, UK
  Tel: +44 (0)1865 776868
Blackwell Publishing Professional, 2121 State Avenue, Ames, Iowa 50014-8300, USA
  Tel: +1 515 292 0140
Blackwell Publishing Asia Pty Ltd, 550 Swanston Street, Carlton, Victoria 3053, Australia
  Tel: +61 (0)3 8359 1011

The right of the Author to be identified as the Author of this Work has been asserted in accordance with
the Copyright, Designs and Patents Act 1988.

First published 2006 by Blackwell Publishing Ltd

2   2008

Library of Congress Cataloging-in-Publication Data
  Eastwood, Sharon.
  Business management for the equine industry / Sharon Eastwood, Anne-Lise Riis Jensen and Anna
  Jordon.
    p. cm.
  Includes bibliographical references and index.
  ISBN-10: 1-4051-2606-X (pbk. : alk. paper)
  ISBN-13: 978-1-4051-2606-9 (pbk. : alk. paper)
  1. Horse industry–Great Britain–Management. 2. New business enterprises–Great Britain.
  I. Jensen, Anne-Lise Riis. II. Jordon, Anna. III. Title.

  HD9434.G7E37 2005
  636.1′068–dc22
  2005004766

ISBN 978-1-4051-2606-9

A catalogue record for this title is available from the British Library

The publisher's policy is to use permanent paper from mills that operate a sustainable forestry policy,
and which has been manufactured from pulp processed using acid-free and elementary chlorine-free
practices. Furthermore, the publisher ensures that the text paper and cover board used have met
acceptable environmental accreditation standards.

For further information on Blackwell Publishing, visit our website:
www.blackwellpublishing.com

Contents

Preface

The equine industry is a huge and complex beast. It combines aspects of the leisure, entertainment and service sectors and draws its customers from all geographic areas and social backgrounds. The one link that every individual business shares is that, in some way, they all draw their income from the horse.

As the horse owning consumer becomes more demanding and the outside influences facing the industry become more pressing there will inevitably be changes in the way in which equine enterprises do business.

This book is designed to fill the gap that exists between stable management and business management books. It does not pretend to provide any business with all the answers. What it does is show business managers not only where to look but also what sort of questions to ask.

By examining the industry as it is now and then looking at current business management and planning theories this book makes useful suggestions as to how these management tools can be applied to equine business.

Because of both the size and diverse nature of the equine industry it would be beyond the scope of this book to examine the detailed ins and outs of every type of enterprise. The particular issues and problems relevant to a farrier are very different from those that affect saddlers or livery yards. It is also very hard to generalise about individual businesses within the industry because they are so diverse.

It is also essential to point out that a text book cannot replace professional advice and that if the reader is in any doubt about a business matter, particularly one of a legal nature, they should consult an appropriately qualified expert.

Acknowledgements

This book would not have been possible without the input of many people, other than the authors. It seemed like an extremely good idea to take our business experience and the research we carried out as part of our MBA studies and convert this into a book which we hope will be useful to others within the equine industry. It has been an interesting journey and many thanks must go to those who have endured our journey with us.

On a technical note, grateful thanks go to Mr Ashley Ede, Equine Industry Lecturer, Mr Gareth Thomas, Economics Lecturer, and Mr Luis Aguiar, Marketing Lecturer, all at the Royal Agricultural College. They have kept our theoretical comments on the straight and narrow.

Thanks also to Denise Ranger at Bentley-Jennison Accountants in Swindon for her supervision of comments on bloodstock accounting.

Finally, to Richard Miles at Blackwell for believing in us at the start, and to the rest of the editorial and publishing staff, thank you.

Abbreviations

ABRS	Association of British Riding Schools
AONB	Area of Outstanding Natural Beauty
BD	British Dressage
BE	British Eventing
BEF	British Equestrian Federation
BETA	British Equestrian Trade Association
BEV	British Equestrian Vaulting
BEVA	British Equine Veterinary Association
BHB	British Horseracing Board
BHDTA	British Horse Driving Trials Association
BHEST	British Horseracing Education and Standards Trust
BHS	British Horse Society
BRHA	British Reining Horse Association
BSJA	British Showjumping Association
DEFRA	Department for Environment, Food and Rural Affairs
DIY	Do it yourself (livery)
DTI	Department of Trade and Industry
EGB	Endurance Great Britain
ERDP	England Rural Development Programme
EU	European Union
FEI	Fédération Equestre Internationale
HGV	Heavy goods vehicle
ICHL	Industry Committee (Horseracing) Ltd
IHT	Inheritance tax
ILPH	International League of Protection for Horses
JAGB	Jockeys Association of Great Britain
JC	Jockey Club
MBA	Master of Business Administration
MOT	Ministry of Transport
NJC	The National Joint Council for Stable Staff
NPS	National Pony Society

NTF	National Trainers Federation
NVQ	National Vocational Qualification
PAYE	Pay as you earn
PCUK	Pony Club UK
PEST	Political, economic, social, technological: the PEST analysis
PPORA	Point to Point Owners and Riders Association
RIABS	Racing Industry Accident Benefit Scheme
RCA	Race Course Association
ROA	Racehorse Owners Association
SEA	Scottish Equestrian Association
SLA	Stable Lads Association
SSSI	Site of Specific Scientific Interest
SWOT	Strengths weaknesses opportunities threats
TBA	Thoroughbred Breeders Association
UK	United Kingdom
USA	United States of America
VAT	Value added tax

1 Overview

So where to start? 'Welcome to the wonderful world of equine business management' sounds a bit dramatic, but at least it lets you know what you are in for. This book contains an introduction to the academic theories of business management and how they relate to the equine industry in the UK. The process of business management has been described in many ways. It has been called a journey, a mission, a battle and even an elephant. It has never yet been compared to a horse, although this is not a bad analogy. A business can be rewarding, frustrating, expensive, time consuming and blessed with a mind of its own. The comparisons are endless.

THE EQUINE INDUSTRY

It makes sense to start at the beginning. Without understanding the industry as a whole, it would be practically impossible to work out where your business fits, and for that matter where your customers come from. The equine industry can be divided and subdivided into a frightening number of individual fragments but unless you can see how the fragments fit back together you will never fully understand the industry of which you are a part.

At the centre of the industry are the manufacturers, the people who produce the raw materials that the rest of us make use of. By raw materials we do not just mean timber and grain we mean the whole range of manufactured products; clothing, rugs, feed, drugs and horses because horses are after all the foundation of the industry.

Next we come to the users, the owners, the riders and the organisations to which they belong. The people who make use of the horse and all the products that go with it. They are a diverse group with interests that range from recreational hacking to Olympic level competition but they all share one thing, the horse is still the focus of their attention.

Then we come to the service providers. The people who 'do' things; the farriers, the vets, the instructors, the grooms and the livery yards. They are possibly the widest group of all but they are still linked by one common denominator, the horse.

For an industry that has grown up around a single species it has an amazingly complex structure and complicated hierarchy but whichever section you find yourself working in you cannot escape the effects and influences of the other sections.

THE LIVERY INDUSTRY

Because the livery yard is the one type of enterprise that almost every other equine business comes into contact with, it makes sense from the point of view of this text to use it as the 'generic' business. We have chosen four hypothetical livery yards as our case studies to illustrate the business issues being faced by various sizes of equine business. It has therefore been necessary to go into some detail about the structure of the livery industry in order to make sure that you, the reader, can get the most out of the case studies.

THE EXTERNAL ENVIRONMENT

No business exists in isolation and irrespective of how insular the management try to be they will inevitably be affected by the goings on in the outside world. Whether or not we pay any attention to world affairs is irrelevant, world affairs will have an effect on us. Something as simple as the price of petrol can have a massive effect on every aspect of your business; oil prices can affect the confidence of the stock market, which in turn affects the value of savings funds, this then affects the amount of money your customers have to spend. Not only are you spending more money every time you fill up your car, but your business is making less as well. This circular logic can be applied to a whole host of issues that originate in the external environment and whether you like it or not, the only way that you can prepare yourself for the effect is to understand the cause.

THE COMPETITIVE ENVIRONMENT

When most horse riders think of the competitive environment they picture a showground. This analogy, although not perfect, is not too far from the truth. Just like your horse at a show, your business will face a variety of challenges before it can achieve its goal. Just like the horse, the business must face rivalry from its fellow competitors. It must deal with opposition in the form of new rivals. It must react to the demands of clients and suppliers in the same way that the horse must react to the rider and the judge. In the end, the prize is more worthwhile than a rosette; it is a productive and prosperous business.

THE RESOURCES

A good rider must always understand the capabilities of his horse. This holds true for a good business manager. Unless you are familiar with all assets at your disposal, you will not be able to make the most of the opportunities that you encounter. While a horseman may consider courage, sound wind and a bold jump, a business manager must pay heed to finances, land, buildings, vehicles and staff. As any horseman knows, unless the whole package is right, the results will not be forthcoming.

It is not enough, however, to just know what you have got. It is just as important to understand how to keep it running. Without the proper care and attention the best horse in the world will not be able to perform. The same is true of any business. Time spent on maintenance and planning will pay dividends in the end.

STRATEGIC PLANNING

Just as a horse needs a work programme, a business needs a plan of attack. Any competitive rider will understand the need for a comprehensive strategy when aiming for a major competition and yet the number of businesses that have no plan beyond next week is staggering. In the same way that the support team for the competition horse need to know who is responsible for what and when everything is supposed to happen, so do the staff within a business. Without a sensible strategy the business is liable to be left in the starting stalls while its rivals are passing the post.

MARKETING

In the same way that a show horse is at its best in the ring where everyone can see and admire it, so a business needs to be seen to be doing its thing. Unless your potential customers know who you are, what you do and how to contact you, you are wasting your time. A business has many opportunities to show itself off, in the same way that the show horse does. Just by being in the arena and doing its best, it can draw attention to itself. The show horse does not need to place an advert to let the judges know it is there, however it does need a good show and some ringcraft. The business can also benefit from forward planning and finesse; there are always ways to promote what you do, you just have to be prepared to try them.

This may seem like a light-hearted and tongue in cheek gallop through business planning but in reality how you conduct yourself in the business environment can make the difference between profit and poverty. Although we are not claiming to provide you with a step by step guide to turning your equine business into a gold mine we hope that the following chapters will provide you with the tools you need to better understand what you need to be doing to improve your business.

Part 1
Assessing a Business

2 The British equine industry

The British equine industry is a very large and fragmented entity. The number and variety of interested parties means that it is very difficult to gather accurate data about the industry as a whole, in fact some people would argue that the horse world should not even be considered as a single unit because it has so many facets and satellites.

> In order to understand the concept of the British equine industry it is useful to first consider the meaning of the words themselves: 'BRITISH' meaning of or relating to Great Britain or the United Kingdom; 'EQUINE' meaning of, relating to or affecting horses; and 'INDUSTRY' meaning an activity in which a great deal of time or effort is expended (Pearsall, 1998).

Based on these definitions there can be no disputing the fact that the horse world in the United Kingdom should be considered as an industry, however defining that industry is no easy task and the suggestion that the fragments should be considered separately has some merit. The counter argument maintains that it is very important for any business to look at the big picture; it would, therefore, be inadvisable for any enterprise operating wholly or partly in the equine industry to completely ignore the sections of the industry which it doesn't normally come into contact with. For this reason this chapter will examine the whole industry as a unit in order to get a feel for the overall make up of and the interdependencies that exist in the horse world in this country.

The industry as a unit is mostly concerned with the activities surrounding the use of the horse as a source of recreation and enjoyment. It can be looked at under three main headings:

- Breeding and manufacturing.
- Owners and riders.
- Services.

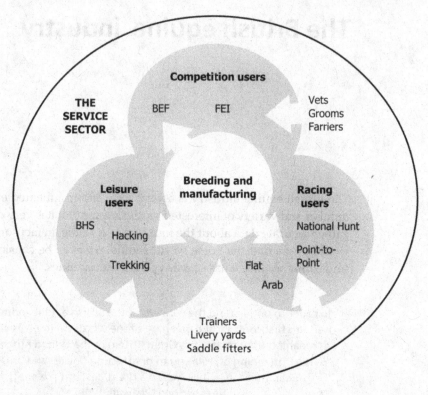

Figure 2.1   The equine industry.

Each of these groups, although focused in their own aims and objectives, is both benefiting from and contributing to the others. And although for ease of understanding we have looked at them separately, it is important to remember that they are linked on many different levels and could not function in isolation (Fig. 2.1).

The arguments regarding the industrial status of the horse world is further complicated by the structure of the industry and the attitudes of the businesses within it. Even though the horse world likes to think of itself as an industry, and individual enterprises like to see themselves as businesses, there is an institutional problem with seeing the horse as a business asset with a monetary value.

> The overall value of the entire horse industry has been estimated at £2.5 billion. The total area of land tied up in the industry, including equine food production, is approximately 500 000 ha and it is second only to farming as a land based rural industry (Houghton Brown, 2001).

Whatever the attitude of the individual people concerned there is no arguing with the fact that there are a large number of people with a large volume of money tied up in horses in one way or another and this money is of primary importance to the rural economy.

The British Equestrian Trade Association (BETA) survey of 1999 provides the most complete data on the industry as a whole. It states that that there are approximately 2.4 million riders and 6000 businesses engaged in equine activities in the UK. It also notes that although equestrianism is an important economic activity, which attracts a large and diverse number of participants, it is difficult to gather accurate data for a number of reasons. These include:

- The participants are widely scattered both demographically and geographically.
- The industry caters for not only the riders themselves but also their horses and helpers.
- There are a number of highly specialised sectors crossing many levels of expertise in several disciplines.
- Professional establishments often engage in several areas on behalf of different categories of owners who themselves often engage in several activities.

MANUFACTURING AND BREEDING

The core components of the equine industry, in our view breeding and manufacturing, are central to all other activities. Without a horse being 'manufactured', the remainder of the industry would be obsolete. We will consider the traditional explanation of manufacturing to be those companies that take raw materials and produce a finished product for supply to the retail market. We will then look at the breeding of the horse in more detail as being a critical element of the equine industry.

The manufacturing sector

Of all the wide variety of equine businesses, manufacturers have more ties with the 'outside' world. The majority of manufacturers, because they are dealing day to day with other industries, tend to operate on more conventional business lines. Animal drug companies are often subsidiaries of major pharmaceutical companies, feed manufacturers deal with agricultural producers. Other areas that come under this sector include horse boxes, stables, fencing, arenas, bedding and equipment such as horse walkers and equine therapy devices.

Dodson & Horrell have been manufacturing horse feed in the UK for over 60 years. They have a comprehensive quality control process and monitor both ingredients and finished products. All cereals are supplied by local farmers and are grown to strict specifications.

The overall growth within the equine industry as a whole is reflected within the manufacturing sector and some manufacturers from other industries have seen it as a suitable area in which to expand; this is particularly apparent in clothing manufacture, with companies like Musto, a respected manufacturer of superior sailing clothes, taking a large market share of the equine clothing market. Advances in textile manufacture have led to massive improvements in the apparel available to both horse and rider in respect of safety, durability and fashion. The range of colours and styles now available is almost overwhelming when compared to the range of 10 years ago.

The relationship between an equine business and its suppliers in general will be covered in more detail in the competitive environment chapter but an in-depth examination of equine related manufacturers is beyond the scope of this book.

The breeding sector

When most people consider the horse breeding industry within the UK they will think of the production of thoroughbred racehorses. Because of the popularity of racing, and the financial value attached to the animals themselves, this aspect of the UK breeding industry receives the most attention and we will therefore consider it first.

Thoroughbred breeding

Horse racing in some form is thought to have begun in 4500 BC and is understood to have begun in Britain in 200 AD. The breeding of race-horses began before Homer and the first horses to be raced seriously in Britain were of Roman stock. Arab stallions were introduced after the Crusades and bred to English mares to improve speed and stamina. In the 16th and 17th centuries the royal family began to take an interest in horse racing and the improvement of the breeding stock. Charles I and James I both hunted in the area around Newmarket and Charles II began offering serious purses to the winners of races; he also laid down the rules of racing as we know them today.

The most dominant stallions served as foundation sires of the breed. These were the Godolphin Arabian, the Byerly Turk and the Darley

Arabian. These three bloodlines are the only lines which remain active to this day. In 1791 James Weatherby traced back every pedigree of every horse racing in England and published *The General Stud Book*. Since 1880, only those descended from horses in this list are allowed to be classified and raced as thoroughbreds.

In 2003 there were over 14 000 horses in training of which approximately 10 500 actually raced for total prize money of £95 million.

The breeding of potential racehorses is a major industry in Britain but unlike Ireland it is not directly linked to farming. All thoroughbreds involved in racing have to be registered with Weatherbys but less than half the horses bred to race ever reach the track in the UK. The rest will go straight into the thoroughbred breeding industry, the other sporting disciplines, the racing industry in other countries or the meat market.

Within the hierarchy of the racing industry, the Thoroughbred Breeders Association (TBA) holds responsibility for handling issues related to the breeding of the thoroughbred within the UK. The TBA was formed in May 1917 to fight a ban on racing brought about by the First World War and to provide cereal feedstuff for horses not in military service, especially mares and foals, to ensure continuation of the industry after the war. The TBA represents the British breeders, lobbies government on issues relating to breeding both nationally and internationally and has been part of establishing the Horse Industry Team within the Department for the Environment, Food and Rural Affairs (DEFRA). It holds a seat on the board of the British Horseracing Board (BHB) and deals with issues such as breeders' prizes, health and safety regulations, staff training, regulations on transport of breeding stock through Europe, rural development and grants, employment regulations, availability of veterinary medicines, fallen stock, stud rates, codes of practice for disease prevention and control, stallion parades, stud visits and management courses.

Thoroughbred studs today are big business and receive most of the plaudits for the production of the modern racehorse but the role of the small breeder must not be underestimated. Most breeders own fewer than five mares, however it is the high profile studs, which own the majority of stallions, that attract all the media attention. Because of the scale of their operation they are able to offer 'special deals' to the small breeder. These 'special deals' include foal share schemes, free veterinary treatment and board, free filly return and delayed payment scheme.

The development of the sport horse

For years British riders relied on the thoroughbred breeders to provide us with our international competition horse but it became apparent that while many of the top event horses were still largely thoroughbred in origin the vast majority of top dressage and show jump horses were warmbloods bred in Europe. This has led to a reassessment of British sport horse breeding.

European countries such as Germany and Holland have an established programme for breeding and developing sport horses that has been producing top class horses for many years. Many people in Britain have recognised that, although we have a number of valuable bloodlines and have produced many good horses, we do not have a national programme in place to promote British bred horses, or to monitor their performance.

This does not mean that we have no successful studs and bloodlines in this country. Establishments such as the Catherston and Welton studs have been producing top class sport horses for many years and their most famous stallions, Dutch Courage and Welton Apollo, have had a lasting impact on the British sport horse.

Several initiatives have been put in place, the most recent of which is the British Equestrian Federation (BEF) breeding and database programme that has taken on the promotion and development of the British sport horse since 2002 (www.bef.co.uk/britishbreeding). This combined the efforts of the British Horse Foundation (established in 1991) and the Supporters of British Breeding (established in 1996) and has two main aims:

- To produce British bred horses capable of taking British international riders to success at the highest level.
- To create an industry-wide initiative to advance the whole of British sport horse breeding.

It has set up several initiatives to take these aims forward, details of which can be found on the BEF website, including the National Equine Database, which will be set up in conjunction with the issuing of equine passports.

Native pony breeding

British native ponies come in a variety of shapes, sizes and colours but share characteristics that are the envy of pony breeders all over the world; they are hardy, versatile and adaptable. These traits have lead to breeding stock from all the breeds being exported as far afield as Australia and the United States. Some enterprising studs have made use of artificial insemination technology to enable them to improve stock without actually shipping ponies halfway around the world.

Breeding and showing native ponies is a popular activity in Britain with the best ponies being shown at local, county and national level. The National Pony Society (NPS) was formed in 1893 and cares for the native pony breeds of the UK but each breed has its own breed society and runs its own shows and pony grading (www.nationalponysociety.org.uk). The breed standards recognise those characteristics that were originally prized by the local inhabitants and are strictly adhered to today.

OWNERS AND RIDERS

The one thing that unites all breeders is the fact that, however wonderful a foal looks on paper, it is valueless unless it has a job to do. In this the breeder is reliant on the end user to produce and develop the raw material. These end users can be divided into three categories:

- Competition and sport.
- Racing.
- Recreation and pleasure.

Each category has its own rules, regulations and traditions and although there is a significant level of interaction and cross over between the memberships there is very little communication of data and almost no co-operation between them. This state of affairs means that it is very difficult to get accurate data regarding the industry as a whole. This fact complicates matters when lobbying government on the issues that affect it.

Although it can reasonably be argued that the owner and the rider are the users, it is impossible to consider the different categories of user without also acknowledging the regulatory bodies that oversee the different activities. The racing and sporting categories must also keep in mind the fact that they are, to a certain extent, providing a service to the watching public. For this reason the spectators and regulators have been examined in this section of the chapter.

Competition and sport

It is easy to think of the sport sector of the industry as being limited to the three Olympic sports: dressage, showjumping and eventing. In reality there is a huge variety of competitive activities that involve horses and all contribute to the overall make up of the industry.

Each activity has its own governing body which determines the rule structure and organisational framework within which the sport functions. Each governing body caters specifically for its own membership and their competitive needs. Communication and data sharing between the organisations is limited; as a result of this they have a less effective political voice than would be expected from the combined number of riders that they represent.

From a business manager's perspective it is important to understand the whole arena within which their business operates. This means that they need to be aware of both the good and bad points of the organisational frameworks which form the boundaries that control aspects of their external environment.

As with any major sporting activity there is a general hierarchical structure to the organisation. However, as with many organisations of this type, below the top layers the interactions and relationships of the groups become confused as the individual interests of the memberships both diverge and mingle.

The Fédération Equestre Internationale

The FEI (www.horsesport.org/fei) is the international governing body of equestrian sport. It was founded in 1921 and has been based in Lausannne (Switzerland) since 1991. It has 130 member countries in 5 continents. It establishes the rules and regulations for the conduct of international equestrian events including the supervision and maintenance of the health and welfare of the horses. It is responsible for dressage, eventing, showjumping, driving, vaulting, reining and endurance disciplines. Its mission is to promote the growth of equine sport worldwide by regulating and administering humane and sportsmanlike international competition.

The British Equestrian Federation

The BEF (www.bef.co.uk) is the liaison between British horse sport and the international community and is affiliated to the FEI. The BEF was set up in 1972 as the senior co-ordinating body for the British Horse Society (BHS) and the British Showjumping Association (BSJA). It now has 12 members and represents over 165 000 riders in Britain. It co-ordinates the UK calendar of international events, disciplinary procedures and doping control, and oversees the training of international judges, stewards, vets and course designers. Through its member organisations the BEF represents both competitive and recreational riders. It plays an active role in representing the common interests of its member bodies to organisations such as the British Olympic Association, the Sports Association, the Farrier Council and the Worshipful Company of Saddlers. Applications for Lottery funding are made by member organisations, through the BEF. The Lottery Sports Fund aims to help sports to progress on the World, Olympic and Paralympic stages. Because the majority of participants are involved in the three Olympic sports it is easy to forget that driving, vaulting, endurance and reining are all international sports in their own right.

The British Showjumping Association

The BSJA (www.bsja.co.uk) is the governing body for the sport of showjumping in Great Britain; Northern Ireland has its own association. It aims to maintain and improve the standard of showjumping while encouraging members at all levels to enjoy fair competition over safe and attractive courses. It manages over 2000 shows providing 2800 days of showjumping each year. In 2001 there were approximately 17 900 horses and ponies registered with the BSJA. The BSJA sets the standards for course design and standardisation, judging, entry requirements and qualification at all affiliated shows. Foreign nationals wishing to compete under BSJA rules must satisfy these regulations as well as those of their own association and the FEI but in national competitions the rules of the BSJA take precedence. Horses and ponies are graded according to the monetary value of their winnings and can compete all year round. Classes range from 'British novice', an introductory class for novice horses and riders, to international classes.

British Eventing

British Eventing (BE) (www.britisheventing.co.uk) is the governing body for the sport of horse trials in the UK. A database is maintained on their website where records of both horse and rider are kept and can be accessed by members of the public. Horse trials originated as a method of training cavalrymen but later developed as a sport in its own right. It first came to the attention of the British public at the Olympic Games after the Second World War.

The organisation has many aims, which include to continue the established success in competition, achieve excellent team performances in international competitions, and increase the opportunities for all members to participate. Horses are graded according to a points system with a set number of points awarded for places and levels of performance. Both horse and rider must attain a certain level of performance before they can move up to the next level.

British Dressage

British Dressage (BD) (www.britishdressage.co.uk) is the governing body for the sport of dressage in Great Britain. It aims to improve the standard of riding, training and horsemanship by promoting and regulating dressage, and also to manage the representation of Great Britain in international dressage competitions and advise the British Equestrian Federation on all dressage matters. Like BE, BD maintains a database on their website where results of horses and riders can be found. Horses are graded according to points gained, and points are awarded according to percentage marks gained in each test.

British Horse Driving Trials Association

The BHDTA (www.horsedrivingtrials.co.uk) is the governing body for the sport of horse driving trials in Britain. Competitors must complete a dressage test, cross-country obstacle test and knock down obstacle test. Horse driving trials is unique in that it is the only equestrian discipline where all entrants – be they horse or pony, male or female, and any age over 14 – compete on an equal footing. The sport is open to pairs (two horses abreast), tandem (two horses in line) and teams (four horses in two pairs).

British Equestrian Vaulting

BEV (www.vaulting.org.uk) is the governing body for the sport of vaulting in Britain. The sport involves performing gymnastic moves on a cantering horse, which the vaulters perform singly, in pairs or teams. Vaulting helps build up balance and confidence on the horse, as well as general athletic ability. You don't need to be able to ride to vault, but vaulting can greatly improve your riding skills.

Endurance Great Britain

Endurance Great Britain (www.endurancegb.co.uk) is the governing body for the sport of endurance riding in Great Britain. It was formed during 2001 with the combination of the British Endurance Riding Association and the Endurance Horse and Pony Society, with the Scottish Endurance Riding Club as an affiliated member. It aims to stimulate greater interest and participation in the sport, holding competitive and non-competitive rides throughout the country, holding seminars and training. The involvement of back-up crews means that even non-riding members of the family can take part.

British Reining Horse Association

The BRHA (www.britishreining.co.uk) was formed in 1995 and is the governing body of reining as a sport in Great Britain. It is affiliated to the National Reining Horse Association (NRHA). The phenomenal worldwide growth of the sport has led to it becoming the first Western discipline to gain full FEI recognition; this means that reining will be part of future World and European Equestrian Games.

Scottish Equestrian Association

The SEA (www.equinesport.org.uk/sea/web/) is recognised by Sport Scotland as being the representative body for all equestrian interests in Scotland. Its mission statement is 'To provide Vision for, and give Leadership and Guidance to Equestrian Interests in Scotland. To make Representations as appropriate to Scottish Parliament, other statutory and non statutory bodies'.

Independent sports (unaffiliated to BEF)

The BEF does not have exclusive possession of horse sport in the UK. There are several sports that do not come under its umbrella and these include horse-ball, gymkhana or mounted games, team chasing, hunter trials, showing and polo. These sports all have their own independent rules and organisational structures. The fact that they are not incorporated into the BEF is not a reflection on their popularity.

Polo has been played since before 600 BC but it was not until the 1850s that it came to the attention of the British. The first club formed was the Calcutta Club in 1862, with the first UK club being formed in 1872. The Hurlingham Polo Association (www.hpa-polo.co.uk) was formed in 1874. It is the governing body for polo in the UK and Ireland as well as for many parts of the Commonwealth and liaises with similar associations throughout the world. Its website contains details of both registered players and clubs.

Racing

The 'Sport Of Kings', as horse racing is colloquially known, is sometimes said to owe its existence to King Charles II who, as a serious racing enthusiast, first set up a racing presence in Newmarket in 1634. However, the origins of the sport go back much further. The first horse races were informal wagers between two owners who each believed their horse to be the fastest.

The three main categories of horse race in Britain are:

(1) Flat: this is where horses compete over a variety of distances, with no obstacles. The race is started with all the horses in 'stalls', to ensure an even break. The Newmarket Town Plate, which was started in 1664, is the oldest recorded race in the racing calendar, where the prizes ranged from a box of cigars to a pack of sausages, and still runs in the first week of October. The best-known flat race with the most coveted title is the Derby held at Epsom in June. Races are classified according to age, sex of horse, distance, handicap by weight and performance and more recently by colour (as a publicity stunt there is an all grey race held at Newmarket).

(2) National Hunt: this is where horses compete over obstacles. These can be either hurdles or steeplechase fences. The best-known hurdle race is The Champion Hurdle held at Cheltenham in March, and the best-known steeplechase is the Grand National held at Aintree in April. They tend to be over a longer distance than flat races, with the horses beginning to jump hurdles in the August of their three-year-old season. Classification is otherwise similar to flat racing.

(3) Point-to-Point: this is racing over obstacles for the amateur rider. Horses are not allowed to be currently racing 'under rules', although at present the horse has to qualify by hunting a prescribed number of days and does have to be registered with Weatherbys. The Point to Point Owners and Riders Association (PPORA) coordinates the meetings, registration of owners, horses and riders. The races themselves are run by individual hunts.

It is important to remember that although Flat, National Hunt and Point-to-Point are the most widely recognised forms of racing in the UK, there are other forms of racing which include Arab racing, harness racing and pony racing.

(4) Arab racing: Arab racing in the UK is an amateur sport featuring races for purebred, part bred and Anglo Arabs which are held at racecourses around the UK. Although amateur in status, they are

run 'professionally' under Jockey Club rules. The two main organisations are the Arab Horse Society (www.arabhorsesoc-uk.com) and the Arabian Racing Organisation (www.arabianracing.org.uk).

(5) Harness racing: this is a massive sport in USA, Australia, New Zealand and Europe and is growing in popularity in the UK. Horses trot or pace at speed while pulling a one seat, two wheel vehicle known as a sulky, around an oval shaped track which is $1/2$ mile in circumference. The horses used are known as standard bred and their gait is either a trot (diagonal trot pace) or a pace (parallel trot pace). Racing speeds get up to 30 mph. In its current form it began in around 1554 but the sport can trace its origins back to chariot racing when it was an Olympic sport with either two or four horses. Chariot racing met its demise with the fall of the Roman Empire. In its more modern form the early records date from 1554. For more details see www.website.lineone.net/~harnessracing-uk.com.

(6) Pony racing: there is a wide variety of types of pony racing practised in the UK today. They range from the Shetland Pony Grand National series which has been a popular part of the Olympia Horse Show for a number of years, through events like the New Forest Point-to-Point which runs across the open forest every Boxing Day, to the form of pony racing which The Pony Club has recently introduced. This takes its lead from an established practice in Ireland to encourage a healthy interest in the art of race riding. Riders are aged between 11–15 and must be members of the Pony Club (www.pcuk.org). Tuition is provided before each meeting.

Horse racing as we know it today is a multi-national, multi-million pound operation of interest to a wide range of organisations and individuals. These interested parties, although linked by the sport they are involved with, have separate responsibilities and agendas based on the interests of their members, so it is important to understand that inevitably for every discussion point there will always be a variety of perspectives.

British Horseracing Board

Racing and breeding is a major industry in Britain and is governed by several organisations, with The British Horseracing Board (BHB; www.bhb.org.uk) being the highest authority. There are 13 members on the Board, comprising 10 voting members and 3 non-voting. The voting members are representatives from The Jockey Club, The Racecourse

Association, The Racehorse Owners Association, The Thoroughbred Breeders Association and The Industry Committee (Horseracing) Ltd plus a chairman, two independent directors and two executives. The non-voting members are expert practitioners from the Racecourse Association and the National Trainers Federation, plus a representative from the race planning committee.

The responsibilities of the BHB are wide ranging across the racing sector and include setting the fixture list, race planning, marketing and promotion of racing, encouraging breeding of bloodstock, training and education programmes, improving the financial position, collection and control of funds required for the administration of racing, and setting the strategic plan and policy for racing. They provide a liaison with the Government and the betting industry, and represent British racing abroad.

Weatherbys Group Ltd

Weatherbys is under contract to the BHB and provides administrative services to racing as well as keeping the *General Stud Book*. It is the largest Passport Issuing Organisation (PIO) in the UK and handles thoroughbred horses in the UK plus a number of horses for the non-thoroughbred register. It publishes *The Stallion Directory* and the *Racing Calendar*, a publication that holds all the races, allowing trainers to choose in which race they wish to enter their horses. Account holders can utilise the online services to enter races and take advantage of the financial and travel services available. Weatherbys administers the entry fees, prize money and riding fees through the member's account. Race cards are printed and distributed daily to racecourses. See www.weatherbys-group.com.

Jockey Club

The Jockey Club (JC; www.thejockeyclub.com) was founded in 1771, confirmed by Royal Charter in 1970 and until 1993 had sole responsibility for governing racing. The formation of the BHB now means the JC is now the regulatory body for jockeys, horses, trainers and permit holders, racecourses and point-to-points. It sets and enforces the rules of racing, issues licences and administers the registration of racing participants (owners, horses, trainers, jockeys and stable staff). It is responsible for setting and enforcing the standards of veterinary and medical care, responsible for the integrity of the sport on and off the racecourse and, last but not least, is responsible for the conduct of a day's racing.

Levy Board

The Horserace Betting Levy Board, which was set up in 1963 with the introduction of the Betting, Gaming and Lotteries Act, is responsible for the collection and distribution of funds from off course horseracing betting from bookmakers and the tote, mainly in pursuit of improvement of racing, but also to improve the breeds of horses – not just thoroughbreds – and the advancements or encouragement of veterinary science. The impending abolition of the Levy Board has been postponed until 2006. For more details see www.hblb.org.uk.

Jockeys Association of Great Britain (JAGB)

The JAGB looks after the interests of jockeys from apprenticeship through to retirement. Jockeys ride the racehorses in races and are licensed by the Jockey Club. They go through a professional apprenticeship with a trainer and have to attend a foundation course held at one of the racing schools. The skill, horsemanship and professionalism of the jockey are of great importance to the outcome of each race. They are also involved in schooling and riding the horses on the training grounds as a way of preparing the horses' fitness. Some jockeys enjoy a celebrity status and act as great ambassadors for the sport.

National Trainers Federation (NTF)

Trainers take other people's horses in and prepare them to race. They too have to be licensed by the Jockey Club. A lot of trainers are based round training centres like Newmarket, Lambourn and Middleham where large areas of land are laid out for exercising horses. The NTF is a professional body for licensed racehorse trainers and has a 94% membership. It supplies members with employment guides and gives legal advice and support. It administers the Racing Industry Accident Benefit Scheme (RIABS) and a stakeholder pension scheme for the staff of trainers. An expert practitioner with no voting right represents the NTF on the British Horseracing Board (BHB). It is also a founder member of the European Trainers Federation. For more information see www.racehorsetrainers.org.

Racehorse Owners Association (ROA)

Racehorse ownership is open to everyone. The ROA (www.racehorse-owners.net) was started in 1945 and provides information and advice to racehorse owners. There are 6800 members who each pay an annual subscription of £120. It has a council made up of 20 members and is represented on several committees at the BHB including the Race Planning Committee, the Industry Committee and the Finance Committee. The ROA works with breeders, racecourses, trainers, jockeys and stable lads and has one board member on the BHB with a voting right.

In 2003 there were 9500 registered racehorse owners, involving around 50 000 people through clubs and syndicates. Off course betting generated £8 bn while on course betting generated £100 bn.

Race Course Association (RCA)

The RCA (www.comeracing.co.uk) represents 59 racecourses staging both flat and jump racing: 16 racecourses stage flat races, 24 jump races and 19 are dual purpose. Three of the racecourses are all weather. The RCA is represented on the BHB board with an expert practitioner who is a non-voting member.

In 2004 Britain's 59 racecourses plan to stage 1341 fixtures with 8500 races involving over 80 000 runners. Over six million people go racing in the UK, with horseracing the most televised sport after football on terrestrial television.

Stable Lads Association (SLA)

The SLA is an independent trade union that represents racing's stable staff at all levels. It holds a seat on the Industry Committee (Racing) Ltd, is a trustee of the Racing Industry Accident Benefit Scheme (RIABS) and a board member on the British Horseracing Education and Standards Trust. It negotiates wages and conditions, and represents staff in disputes and disciplinary actions. Membership is free to certain groups of stable staff and is automatic with registration at the Jockey Club. Information is available through the careers page on the NTF website.

The National Joint Council for Stable Staff (NJC)

The NJC is made up of members from the SLA and the NTF to pursue the common objective of efficiency and prosperity of the racing industry, promotion of security of employment and advancement of employees. The NJC also provides a standard contract of employment, setting out minimum terms and conditions with non-contractual disciplinary proceedings to help deal with difficulties and provide arbitration.

British Horseracing Education and Standards Trust (BHEST)

BHEST was established in 1993 and is a registered charity, recognised by government as the awarding body for a number of NVQ qualifications in racing breeding and farriery. It aims to raise standards in the racing and thoroughbred breeding industries through training, education and qualifications. For more information see www.bhtb.co.uk.

Industry Committee (Horseracing) Ltd (ICHL)

The ICHL coordinates the jockeys, stable lads, racecourses, trainers and breeders with one voting board member on the BHB. This vote is in addition to the fact that the RCA, NTF and TBA have their own representation on the BHB.

The recreation sector

The 1999 BETA survey estimated that 80% of the UK's 2.4 million riders are recreational riders. This group of riders is the most difficult to categorise because there is very little accurate data about them, largely due to the huge diversity of interests and habits that they exhibit. There are also many horse owners who belong to no group or organisation and own horses for the simple pleasure of hacking out.

There are, however, several organisations that cater for the recreational rider, some of which come under the jurisdiction of the BEF.

British Horse Society

The BHS (www.bhs.org.uk) was founded in 1947 and is a registered charity. It aims to be the voice of the recreational rider and oversees the training and grading of riding instructors. It performs a valuable service by maintaining and monitoring bridleways and by championing road safety for riders. It also plays an essential role in promoting horse welfare.

In conjunction with the International League for the Protection of Horses (ILPH) and the British Equine Veterinary Association (BEVA) it has introduced a registration scheme for livery yards which will be covered in more detail later on.

The Pony Club

The Pony Club (www.pcuk.org) was founded in 1949, celebrating its 75th anniversary in 2004. Many young recreational and competitive riders are involved in Pony Club activities. It has over 110 000 members in 18 countries. Almost 40 000 belong to one of the 357 branches or 260 centres in the UK. It provides social, competitive and recreational activities for members as well as providing the opportunity to improve riding skills and stable management knowledge.

The Association of British Riding Schools

The Association of British Riding Schools (ABRS; www.abrs.org.uk) was founded in 1954 and is the only organisation representing professional riding school proprietors. It has Britain's longest established riding school approval scheme and aims to promote good standards of horse management and business management. In order to gain approval an establishment must have been inspected and found to be satisfactory by one of the National Approved Schemes. The ABRS sets a high standard for horse care and requires that the instruction given is well-presented and correct in content. The size of the establishment is immaterial; it is the standards that are important. All riding schools, according to law, must hold a licence to operate their business. The licence is granted by local authorities.

Recreational riders are not necessarily horse owners and there is almost no conclusive data about the number of non-horse owning riders active at any one time or the actual frequency of participation. The ABRS is the only organisation affiliated to the BEF which deals directly with this category of horse rider.

Riding clubs

Riding clubs have the choice of being affiliated to the BHS but it is not compulsory. Although originally intended to offer the advantages of the Pony Club to adult riders, most now cater for the whole family. Although those that are affiliated to the BHS come under the auspices of the BEF, this leaves a segment of the equestrian population that is not covered by any of the major governing bodies.

Trekking centres

Riding holidays are becoming increasingly popular and this has led to a boom in the trekking sector of the leisure industry. Although this sector of the industry makes an important contribution to the industry as a whole, the particular group of riders which it services does not necessarily come under the jurisdiction of any of the major governing bodies, therefore there is little data available. It would, however, be a mistake for the industry as a whole to ignore the contribution made by these riders, some of whom are undoubtedly the horse owners of the future.

THE SERVICE SECTOR

Although in our diagrammatic representation of the industry, services are shown on the outside, they are quite often the interface between the manufacturers and the owners and riders. A racehorse owner relies on his trainer to get the most enjoyment out of his horse. Without the services of an equine vet, the majority of horse owners would not have the skills and understanding to utilise the drugs and equipment available. The service sector is therefore a vital part of the industry as a whole.

Any business providing a service needs to be aware of its relationship with customers and suppliers, in order to maximise its revenue and minimise its costs. Some service providers within the equine industry tend to specialise in a particular sector, in order that the customer knows who they are dealing with. For example, any vet can do vaccinations, but equine clients tend to prefer an experienced equine vet when dealing with problems. An established farrier may decide to concentrate on surgical shoeing, while another may decide to work within the racing sector.

The British Equestrian Trade Association (BETA; www.beta-uk.org) works to support its members in their efforts to achieve the highest level of repute, knowledge and profitability. Originally formed in 1979 by Anthony Wakeham with 30 members, it now has over 600 members with a group turnover of £2 million. It is involved in political lobbying on issues such as hunting, VAT on hats and horses, and European legislation on veterinary medicine. It provides a range of services for its members including business training, discounted insurance and other concessions. The most relevant report on the equine industry was produced by BETA in association with the Produce Studies Group, providing details on consumer spend, levels of satisfaction and numbers of horses within the UK.

The service sector of the industry is probably the most diverse of all the sectors which includes saddlers, retailers, vets, farriers, instructors, livery yards and other specialist personnel; in fact, any business which provides a service to the owners, riders, breeders and manufacturers. Because we will be using case studies from the livery industry to illustrate many of the business situations discussed within this book, we will be analysing the livery industry in more detail in the next chapter. This does not reflect the relative importance of this part of the service sector compared to the other service providers.

3 The livery industry

Although this book is not solely geared towards the livery industry it is inevitable that the first equine business most people think of is a livery yard. For this reason the illustrative case studies that make up Part 3 of this book will be primarily based on livery yards. It is therefore necessary to examine this particular area in more detail.

A livery yard is, broadly speaking, a boarding house for horses. There are a huge number of livery enterprises ranging from small DIY yards to large, purpose built full and competition establishments all over Britain and there has been an increase in demand for livery places over the last few years. Because there is no compulsory national register of livery yards it is impossible to gauge the number of yards or horse places accurately. These factors combine to make it very difficult to construct an accurate picture of the status quo in this sector of the industry.

DEFRA minister Elliot Morley recently highlighted the fact that while catteries and kennels have to be licensed, livery yards do not. He has suggested that this may change with the modernisation of the Protection of Animals Act but a government enforced approval scheme could have far reaching consequences for the equine industry as a whole.

In 2002 the BHS launched a voluntary scheme to approve livery yards. The scheme is designed not only to increase and maintain standards in existing yards but also to provide help for anyone setting up a new yard. Yards are expected to cover the cost of an inspection and pay an annual registration fee. Livery yard owners are offered support and advice, and are made aware of any changes in law that affect them. The scheme offers horse owners someone to complain to and someone who can act as a mediator in the event of a dispute.

While there is an exceptionally good bush telegraph within the industry there is no accurate data on average costings or expected profits and horse people are notoriously bad at keeping accurate figures or projecting realistic incomes. This means that there is very little basis for comparison when trying to estimate the profitability of a new or existing enterprise. Large numbers of livery enterprises are also built into existing enterprises and make use of pre-existing assets. It is therefore difficult to calculate the accurate income and expenditure of many of the small equine businesses in existence.

RANGE OF SERVICES AVAILABLE

The livery sector of the horse world can be further subdivided into different types of service ranging from the elite full hunter and competition livery to the basic DIY or grass livery. Due to the lack of communication and cohesion of the horse world in general and the fact that most yards offer a range of types of livery, there are no reliable figures on the exact size of each sector of the livery market.

In addition to their primary activity that may be another equine pursuit or an unrelated business such as farming, many yards offer livery services. This state of affairs is further complicated by the fact that many yards offer different packages to suit the season. For example, hunter liveries from August to April, break and school liveries in spring and full competition or polo liveries from April to September. These are often supplemented by grass, part or DIY clients to make up the numbers.

Full livery

Full livery is the term applied to the most comprehensive level of horse care service available. The yard undertakes all the routine care and maintenance of the horse including exercise and fitness work, grooming, trimming and tidying the mane and tail, maintenance and daily care of saddlery and in addition will prepare the horse in full for the owner's chosen activity. This can include specialised schooling, transport to and from events and the maintenance and preparation of equipment. Some types of livery, particularly polo and hunter, can also include the provision of a groom at events.

Full hunter livery is a specific service geared towards hunting people. The yard owner takes full responsibility for all preparation of the horse for the duration of the hunting season as well as basic care while the horse is out of work during the summer. In most cases the animal will be brought into work in June and will be exercised, fed, clipped, plaited and transported to and from the hunt venue by the livery staff. The price per week will cover all the above-mentioned services but will exclude farrier and vet fees. The price varies slightly from yard to yard and there is also some fluctuation between different hunt areas. Typical charges in Hampshire would be lower than in the more prestigious Beaufort (Gloucester and Wiltshire) or Quorn (Leicestershire) hunt areas and bills are normally settled monthly.

It is also difficult to gauge the number of yards offering this service as many are small, one man set-ups which are lumped in with farm enterprises and therefore do not exist as businesses in their own right. A large number of hunter livery places are also run as a small add-on to an existing private yard; an individual who keeps their hunters at home will often offer a hunter livery service to utilise any spare stables as a means of covering the cost of their own hunting.

Competition livery

Competition livery is aimed at competitive clients and can vary depending on which discipline the horse and rider specialise in. Many yards will gear their services towards the yard manager's particular area of interest. This gives the client the benefit of a more suitable atmosphere in which to base their horse and allows the yard staff to concentrate on what they know best. As well as the day-to-day care of the horse, the service will include specific skills such as training of the horse and rider, the correct level of fitness for the combination's current aspirations, and preparation and maintenance of all the relevant equipment.

As with hunter livery the client will be billed separately for farrier and vet's fees but, unlike hunter livery, transport is usually billed as an addition. The weekly charge will largely depend on the level of training available; for example it will cost significantly more to keep a horse with an Olympic level trainer than at a standard yard. The charges for a competent level of care without any elite extras (such as an Olympic level trainer) are usually in line with a hunter livery place.

Schooling livery

Break and school liveries are a very specific service available to the owners of young and problem horses. It is a very specialist area of horse care, which is offered at a wide variety of prices by an even wider variety of yards. There is no recognised qualification or accreditation system for people wanting to work on young or difficult horses so the standard of service available can vary greatly. This situation is further complicated by the fact there is no 'one right way' to break in or school horses, and practitioners of the different schools of thought are quick to criticise each others' methods. One method for horse handling is based on the Monty Roberts join-up, and in some cases trainers using these methods can and do charge higher rates.

The break and school service is used by both professional and private clients. Private horse owners without the necessary experience or time to start training their young horse will often choose to send their horse to an experienced professional, and busy yards without the necessary specialist staff will also make use of a yard that specialises in breaking.

Because for many people having a young horse is a one-off experience, the choice of yard can be difficult and most people will select a yard based on a personal recommendation.

Part livery

Part livery as a specific type of livery is difficult to clarify because it comes in many forms. The basic part livery package is where the yard undertakes the day-to-day essential aspects of horse care such as mucking out and tidying the stable, feeding, changing rugs and turning out in the field while the owner is responsible for exercising, care and maintenance of saddlery, grooming, trimming and clipping.

However there are infinite variations of the basic package and many yards will offer individual services and charge daily or weekly for these add-ons. The range of facilities varies greatly from yard to yard, as does the standard of service offered.

DIY livery

Do it yourself (DIY) livery is the basic bare minimum livery. The yard supplies and maintains the stable and grazing and the horse owner is responsible for all aspects of the care and maintenance of the horse.

In most DIY yards the horse owner is responsible for purchasing all the bedding, forage and feed but the yard will provide storage space, although some yards, particularly those on farms, will sell hay, haylage and straw. As with all other types of livery the additional facilities and services offered will vary greatly from yard to yard as will the price structure and billing method.

VARIATION OF CHARGES

As anyone who keeps a horse at livery knows, the variation in livery bills from yard to yard can be staggering. Although this is obviously affected by geographic location and available facilities there are other factors that need to be taken into consideration. There is also no industry standard for what is or isn't included in the basic bill. While some yards may allow clients free use of horse walkers and arenas, others will charge for everything over and above the basic stable. This disparity means that without seeing an itemised bill it is impossible to draw useful conclusions from the vast range of prices charged for livery services.

Part of the problem of comparing livery charges is the difficulty in defining the 'typical' livery yard. Although many yards are run as businesses there is also a large percentage of horse places in private yards. Private stable owners usually offer these livery places to clients as a way of off setting the cost of their own horses. The livery place is often offered at a slightly lower rate than the professional yards in the area and because there are in most areas many horse places of this type it has the effect of capping prices throughout the industry.

The pricing policy for a livery yard has to be made in a competitive context; this means that the fees charged must relate to those being charged by rival establishments. The influence of competition on prices will depend on both the number and strength of competitors within the market. In other words the amount of money that you as a business can charge for what you provide is to a certain extent dictated by the other businesses competing for your clients' money.

> In the majority of business situations the standard method for setting a price structure is to work out how much a product or service will cost your business to provide; this will give you your break-even price. You then add on a suitable profit margin to arrive at the final price (Nellis and Parker, 2002).

Because of the inter-yard socialisation that occurs out hunting and at competitions, horse owners tend to be well informed as to what other yards in the area are charging. This leads to a certain amount of pressure being exerted on yard owners to not charge significantly more than their competitors without reasonable justification. This is what is known in economic theory as perfect competition; everybody knows what everybody else is doing, the individual businesses and clients are too small to in any way distort the market, yards have similar products and there is nothing to prevent a new yard from opening in the area. However, some yards are fortunate enough to be in a 'monopolistic' situation; they have no immediate rivals and therefore have a captive audience. This means that, within reason, they can charge what they like. This status quo can only be maintained if there is something preventing new business starting up nearby, such as planning legislation and land prices (Nellis and Parker, 2002).

The *Equine Business Guide* is the best source of facts and figures available to the equine industry (Bacon, 2002). It provides financial and statistical data on a range of equine businesses. The guide relies on individual businesses providing the data that goes into the finished guide and acknowledges that the quality of the final analysis is determined by the volume and quality of the data supplied. It also points out in the opening chapter that there are several factors that must be considered when comparing enterprises:

- All businesses operate within their own individual set of circumstances and therefore have unique cost and income structures.
- The size of the yard is likely to have an impact on the fixed costs per horse.
- The number of horses contributing to the profits, i.e. not belonging to the owner's family, will also have an impact.

Livery yard owners do not, as a rule, increase their prices on a regular basis. Fees tend to be left for several years and then increased by a significant amount instead of rising by a sensible amount every year. This means that horse owners get a good deal for a few years until it is absolutely necessary for the yard owner to raise the fees, they then get a shock increase which makes up for the last few years' price freeze. Yard owners justify this by saying that owners will not tolerate an annual rise but then get defensive when clients complain about the large increase. Initial discussions between prospective client and owner will cover the current price but often allow no provision for future price increases.

The other factor that affects what a yard can charge for its services is the elasticity of the demand. This refers to how responsive the demand for the service is in relation to other factors. A demand that is said to be highly elastic will be significantly affected by a very small change whereas an inelastic demand will not. There are two key 'elasticities' that need to be considered within the livery industry: price elasticity and income elasticity.

The *price elasticity of demand* relates to how much the demand for the service will change as the price changes. While the demand for less essential or more widely available services offered such as lessons and clipping is very sensitive to price increases, the demand for core services such as stable and grazing is less so.

Price elasticity is affected by several factors: product differentiation, available substitutes, proportion of income that is involved in the purchase, perceived value, complementary nature of the product and the 'prestige value' of the product (Lipsey and Chrystal, 1999).

The *income elasticity of demand* relates to the responsiveness in the level of demand to a change in the client's income. It can be determined by the degree of necessity attributed to the product or service. In other words a luxury or indulgence, such as made to measure riding boots, is likely to be much more sensitive to a drop in income than a necessity, such as a riding hat. To an industry outsider the horse itself may be seen as a luxury item and the logical conclusion to this is that the demand for all things equine is highly elastic. In reality most horse owners will acknowledge that their horses are considered as part of the family and so, although the demand for items such as new saddles and smart rugs is sensitive to income, the demand for essentials such as vets bills, livery bills and shoes is much less so. The essential factor for a livery yard to consider is the level of service that it provides because while removing the horse and placing it somewhere cheaper is a fairly drastic step, dropping from full livery to part or DIY is a logical reaction to a drop in available income.

FACILITIES OFFERED

The variety and standard of facilities offered by livery yards is as diverse as the services that they offer. There is a general trend within the industry that the higher the level of service that is offered the more extensive the range of facilities that is made available to the clients. However, as horse owners become more demanding there is a steady swing towards better facilities in all types of yard.

Fifteen years ago it was unusual to find anything but the most basic facilities in a DIY yard but, with the increase in tack, trailer and horse theft as well as the distressing series of equine mutilations that take place periodically, there has been a general move towards better supervision and security in most yards. This change has been driven not only by the demands of the customer but also at the insistence of the insurance industry.

Although it is not surprising to find that the yards offering the higher levels of service have a wide range of facilities, a recent small-scale survey of facilities available showed that the biggest range of facilities was not just restricted to the top end of the market. Of the horse owners questioned 57% kept their horses at DIY establishments yet the majority of them had access to as wide a variety of facilities as the respondents from the more expensive end of the market.

The level of traffic today means that riders are now more wary of riding on the roads. Good hacking has always been an important factor when choosing a yard but more and more riders now appreciate an all weather arena as an alternative way to exercise their horse. An arena is no longer seen as a luxury for competition riders but is increasingly viewed as a major advantage, particularly during the winter when fields are too wet to ride in and it is too dark to venture on to the roads. As livery yards are forced to compete for clients the level of facilities will become increasingly important.

Clients expect good grazing with suitable fencing and space to store feed, bedding and tack; it is the add-ons that yards can use as a unique selling point, such as horse walkers, coffee rooms and arenas.

The external environment

4

In order to understand the workings of an industry it is important to get a feel for all the factors that influence it. The term 'external environment analysis' when used in a business context means exactly what it says. It is the examination of those external factors which affect the environment within which a business functions. The macro environment consists of all the outside influences that impact on the day-to-day running of the business. To make analysis easier it can be further divided into the competitive environment and the external environment. The competitive environment will be examined in more detail in the next chapter.

Because we can do very little to influence these factors it is easy to write them off as being outside our control and therefore not really our problem. Livery yards in particular have a tendency to think of the broader external environment as outside their control and therefore not worth bothering about. It is rare to find a yard manager who understands that although these factors are generally outside their influence the circumstances that they create still have to be managed. This attitude, although common in the equine industry, is by no means unique to it.

> While hiding your head in the sand is a survival tactic that has served many an ostrich well it is not particularly helpful to a business. It is fair to say that it is infinitely easier to react to something that you saw coming than to a bolt from the blue. For this reason it makes good business sense to examine your external environment periodically, in order to have an advanced warning of both storm clouds and patches of sunshine.

From the point of view of advising an enterprise whose manager has no formal business training it is easier to keep the guidelines simple. This does not mean patronising the manager and dumbing down the advice but rather structuring the techniques and frameworks in such a way that they can be related to the industry and business in question.

There are many different types of analysis suggested in management textbooks. Each one concentrates on a particular type of influence and while this can focus the attention of the organisation on the problems in hand it can cause the management to 'think in lists' rather than thinking laterally. It can also encourage the examiner to think in monochrome rather than taking in the full colour picture. It is also important to remember that these analyses only present a snapshot of the way things are currently, but the factors affecting any business are constantly changing.

> The relevance of different influences may change over time and factors relevant to one organisation may not be relevant to another (Johnson and Scholes, 1997).

The 'time sensitivity' of the analysis cannot be over emphasised. The most thorough and careful environmental analysis carried out on 10 September 2001 would have been of very little use two days later because so many of the basic assumptions on which it was based had changed beyond all recognition. Although world-shattering events of this scale are few and far between it is a fact of life that nothing in the business world is absolutely static.

HOW DO WE GET THE INFORMATION?

> For environmental analysis to be effective it is important for the individual business concerned to distinguish between those factors which are vital and those which are merely important (Grant, 2002).

There are no hard and fast rules for the gathering of information. In a corporate environment this may well be accomplished by detective work and industrial espionage but the structure of the livery industry means that everyone knows what everyone else is doing anyway so the information gathering is the easy part.

However, it is also important to bear in mind that by definition 'you can never know which bits of information you don't yet know'. It is a detective film truism that the last bit of knowledge is often the key to the whole plot.

Although gossiping in a canteen or on a show ground is not the most scientific method of generating data it can be unnervingly accurate and will give a good indication of where to start digging, particularly regarding the strengths and weaknesses of competitors. For a wider perspective it is a good idea to examine the industry journals such as *Horse and Hound*. This will give an up-to-date idea of what the industry is thinking, particularly the letters pages where current issues are often debated. For more scientific data gathering it may be necessary to contact government or regulatory bodies.

> For details of government, legislative and legal issues it is advisable to contact organisations such as DEFRA (Department for the Environment, Food and Rural Affairs), BETA and the BHS. They should be in a position to help with sourcing information of this type (www.defra.gov.uk, www.beta-uk.org and www.bhs.org.uk).

FRAMEWORK FOR THE ANALYSIS

Assessing the situation is as much about asking the right questions as analysing the answers. By asking 'How did we get to here?', 'What went right or wrong?' and 'Why did we do that?' we can gain valuable insight into our own actions; this in turn can give us a way of moving from a problem to a solution. However, in answering these questions, it is important to avoid 'analysis paralysis' and to remember that inferences from the past and the present may not automatically be a guide to what might happen in the future. With this in mind it is perhaps more prudent to turn our questioning outwards and start asking 'What's going to happen next?', 'How is it likely to affect us?' and 'Is there any way we can prepare for it?' instead.

Because the external environment is a huge area to try to make sense of it is useful to have some method of structuring the analysis. There are any number of ways in which the data can be divided up but the framework most commonly suggested in management textbooks is the PEST analysis (Fig. 4.1).

> As there are no hard and fast rules governing the analytical process because each analysis needs to be specific to the business concerned, it may be useful to begin the process with a checklist: Political, Economic, Social and Technological, which is often referred to as a PEST analysis (Lynch, 2000).

Some experts recommend that the PEST analysis is expanded to include separate categories for the legal and environmental aspects

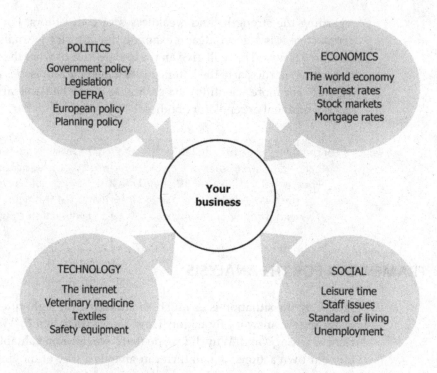

POLITICS

Government policy
Legislation
DEFRA
European policy
Planning policy

ECONOMICS

The world economy
Interest rates
Stock markets
Mortgage rates

Your
business

TECHNOLOGY

The internet
Veterinary medicine
Textiles
Safety equipment

SOCIAL

Leisure time
Staff issues
Standard of living
Unemployment

Figure 4.1   The PEST analysis.

of the external environment. Although these subject areas can be examined under the political and social sections already included in the simpler format, in an industry that has particular legal or environmental factors it makes sense to discuss them as separate subject areas. The PEST analysis thus becomes the PESTLE analysis (L = legal; E = environmental).

This division of factors can be restrictive because some factors will fit into more than one category and may need to be looked at in several contexts. On top of this, some factors are in turn affected by the others. For example the threat to the hunting community is undoubtedly a political issue; however, it also raises some social questions so should be considered in this context as well.

Some factors will not only cross boundaries within one of the analytical frameworks but will also impact on several aspects of the business's environment. The situation that the hunting sector of the industry finds itself in must therefore also be considered as an influence on both the competitive and the internal environments that will be looked at in the next chapter.

It is important to remember that each template is relevant to a particular type of influence so in order to see the big picture it may be necessary to use a combination of methods.

POLITICAL FACTORS

There are many dimensions to the political environment and it is unrealistic to expect a small business to analyse all the potential side effects but it is important to acknowledge the imminent changes that could impact on the business, and develop contingency plans.

The political section covers any changes in the political climate that could have relevance to the industry. It also examines any changes in government policy and legislation that are likely to have a positive or negative effect on the status quo. Until fairly recently the political environment was seen in equine circles as being outside its control and therefore beyond consideration. However the changes in the political climate over the last five years have resulted in a drastic alteration in attitudes throughout the industry.

The political climate is largely dictated by the beliefs of the political party in power; this in turn is affected by the social environment with a time delay caused by the election cycle. The imminent political changes are already causing speculation and anxiety within the industry although they have yet to have an actual impact in many areas of the country. As with many things in life the fear of change is often worse than the change itself.

The hunting ban

The political threat to hunting in the UK was already having a destabilising effect on the equestrian industry several years before the Parliament Act was used. At the current time it is difficult, if not impossible, to predict how far reaching the consequences of such a ban will be.

Although most horse owners do not keep horses solely for the purpose of pursuing hounds, the loss of hunting will have a huge impact on the full and hunter livery business, particularly in the heart of the prime hunt countries such as the Beaufort (Wiltshire and Gloucester), The West Country and the Quorn (Leicester).

407 791 people marched in London in July 2002. The march, organised by the Countryside Alliance, aimed to highlight not just the hunting issue but the strength of feeling within the entire rural community for the Government's lack of understanding of rural issues.

> The BETA submission to the committee of enquiry into hunting estimates that hunting produces £72 million annual turnover and 9259 jobs in the equestrian industry but calculates that the total loss to the industry long term as a result of the ban will be closer to £179.4 million. It states that the real effect of the ban will not be felt for a generation. The hunting ban, although political in origin, will have both economic and social effects on the industry as a whole (BETA, 2002).

Farm diversification incentives

As a response to the current financial problems that many farmers are facing the Government is advocating diversification. Various financial schemes are accessible to farmers wishing to diversify, including grants and partial relief from business rates. The Government has also encouraged planning authorities to approve developments that fit in with the local environment and add to the rural economy as part of the England Rural Development Programme (ERDP).

> Details of the ERDP and other Government incentives are available on the DEFRA website at www.defra.gov.uk

Many farmers had already investigated the possibilities but in order to be sustainable a yard must be situated in an area were there is a genuine need, either through lack of any facilities or lack of quality facilities. The current grant-funded push towards new equine units has, however, the potential to upset the status quo. There is a real danger that the new yards could undercut the existing, established set-ups. This would reduce their profit margins and, far from improving the rural economy, all it would achieve is to spread the incoming funds over more enterprises thus generating a small income for several people rather than a sensible income for one or two.

There have been concerns raised that flooding the market with funding assisted yards could lead to a lowering of standards. However, it is likely that taking into account how fickle the average horse owner can be, the rules of supply and demand will start to take effect. This means that after an initial rush to see if the grass really is greener on the other side of the fence, the market will settle down with the good yards surviving and the weaker yards dropping out. This is more likely to result in a raising of standards as the competition for clients gets tougher. Although this is not so good for the farmer struggling to make some extra profit on a few stables it is a healthy state of affairs for the horse industry as a whole.

Compulsory registration for livery yards

If the current BHS voluntary registration scheme is replaced by a compulsory government scheme it could have wide reaching implications for many yards. There is a danger that yards would have to invest heavily in order to bring their facilities up to the recommended standard and, as has been seen in other industries, this type of mandatory expenditure could push smaller yards out of business.

ECONOMIC FACTORS

The economic environment, by its very nature, has a more immediate effect on people within the industry even though they may not recognise it as one of the key external influences.

Any factors that affect the amount of money in the British economy can and do exert an influence on business. Both interest and exchange rates impact on an individual's feeling of financial security and this will have an effect on both the availability of and the attitude towards spending disposable income. While it is unlikely that a drop in disposable income will lead to people selling their horses there is a real danger that they will cut down on equine expenses such as full and competition livery.

The economic factors are both affected by and are beyond the control of government because our own economy is linked to the global economy.

National minimum wage

The changes in legislation regarding the national minimum wage originate in the political section of this analysis but because the results are purely economic they will be considered in this section. This factor is a double-edged sword. It will have an impact on labour costs in many yards that will then have to pass this increased cost on to the clients in order to maintain their gross margins. It could also affect the clients themselves, either by increasing their income if they are employees or by decreasing their profits if they are employers.

Stock markets

The relative health of the stock market may not have an immediate effect on an individual's financial security but it will alter the value of savings and pension funds, which will have some effect on an individual's spending habits. It can, however, have a large and immediate effect on individuals whose main income is tied to the markets, either through employment in a trading house or through private investments.

Interest rates

The interest rate will have a more immediate impact on spending habits than the stock market because it will have an instant effect on mortgage and loan repayments. This will affect overnight the amount of disposable income available to horse owners and therefore needs to be recognised by yard owners as an important influence on their incomes. It also has an effect on the business owners themselves if they have any repayments to make. They will need to be aware that just increasing prices is not a sensible option if their clients are already feeling the pressure from their own borrowing, so they will need to think of other ways of generating revenue.

The low interest rate that investors are currently enjoying means that many people have stretched their borrowing limits to enable them to purchase property or fund lifestyle improvements. This level of borrowing is sustainable while the interest rate remains low but could have severe implications for many homeowners if the base rate rises significantly.

The world economy

The economic climate tends to have a less immediate effect on the DIY sector of the market because the horse owners at this level tend to be genuine enthusiasts who see their animals more as part of the family than as an extravagance. The key question here could well be 'Is the industry itself actually set to grow in view of the fact that horses are considered to be a luxury and the world economy is currently in a state of flux?' The answer to this question is beyond the scope of most equine businesses because they do not have access to this level of financial analysis but it is still a factor that needs to be considered, if only in a 'If the worst happens can we cope?' sort of way.

Increase in disposable income

The increase in disposable income that this generation enjoys is linked with the increase in leisure time, which will be considered under social influences and is generally held to be responsible for the rise in equestrianism as a recreational pastime. The industry as a whole needs to be aware that there is no guarantee that this state of affairs will continue indefinitely.

As has been mentioned under the 'variation of charges' section of Chapter 3 the relationship between income and price structures has already been examined but that is not the only way in which a client's income can affect a yard. The business manager also needs to be aware of the possible effects should either the political or other economic factors alter this situation.

SOCIAL FACTORS

Social influences can be hard to assess because they are, at a very basic level, the attitudes of the general public.

The attitude of the population to the industry can have a huge impact on the health of the industry. Whether an activity is considered trendy or not will, to a certain extent, govern how much new investment is available. The current economic climate, the political stability and the media can affect the attitudes of the populous. They can in turn, through the democratic process, have an effect on the political environment, which can have a knock on effect on the economic environment.

It is important to realise that although social trends do not change overnight they can change considerably over a number of years. The current social attitudes towards foxhunting are a good example of this phenomenon.

Expected standard of living

Today's society enjoys a generally higher standard of living than previous generations. The current trend away from manual labour and towards white-collar employment has led to changes in expectations and aspirations. A career with horses is not nearly as appealing as it was 20 years ago largely due to the increased options open to school leavers in the new century.

There is a current social trend towards a healthy lifestyle and enjoying the great outdoors, and riding as an activity, particularly through the 'Jeep National Riding Festival', is cashing in on this. Whether the rate of recruitment can be maintained and the new converts can be persuaded to stay remains to be seen.

Increase in leisure time

As leisure time increases, owning a horse for relaxation and pleasure becomes a more attractive proposition for many people. The increased availability of arenas and improved competition facilities mean that horse owners are not as restricted by the hours of daylight as they once were and are able to participate in a wide range of activities without having to travel excessive distances.

Employment figures

The level of unemployment within the economy will have a dual effect on the equine industry. If unemployment is high then it should become easier for yards to find staff because there will be more young people looking for employment. However high unemployment leads to feelings of financial insecurity which will affect the clients' attitude to spending their disposable income and will therefore alter the economic environment within which the business functions.

Staff issues

The increasing staff crisis that the equestrian industry is facing is a multi-faceted problem. It is becoming progressively harder for employers to find staff to fill both junior and senior positions because the quantity and quality of applicants at both ends of the spectrum seem to be slowly declining.

There is a definite shortage of young entrants into the 'hands on' areas of the industry although the seemingly more glamorous yards have less trouble recruiting young staff members. This may not just be due to the 'glamour' but to the fact that a successful yard has the ability to provide a higher standard of working conditions. The chance to work with an equestrian celebrity, coupled with the opportunity to travel, will ensure a supply of young grooms to the higher-level competition yards. Yards with a respected reputation also have a greater chance of attracting staff because of the value that their references have to a CV. It is therefore the less prestigious yards that are feeling this particular squeeze the most, although it is not exclusively their problem.

The loss of experienced staff is a huge problem to the industry and is being felt by all the 'hands on' sectors. There are a number of reasons why a groom decides to pursue a different career but the long hours and difficult pay structure can influence the decision.

Although the lack of young staff is a complex problem with causes outside the control of the industry, the loss of experienced personnel is largely the fault of the industry itself. If experienced personnel are to be kept they must be valued. This means that they need to receive the levels of respect and payment that other comparable professions enjoy.

TECHNOLOGICAL FACTORS

This section covers both recent and potential technological advances that impact on the industry and at first glance it can be difficult to find the technological aspects of an industry that is based entirely around a four legged mammal that evolved into its current form several hundred years ago.

Technological influences are not just those that affect the industry in question but also those that affect the standard of living of the population at large. This includes both recent and potential technological advances. Technological issues can in turn affect the social issues as increases in global communication lead to increased social awareness.

The internet revolution has affected all aspects of society, and recent developments in textiles have been put to good use in the rug industry. There is also the advance in all weather surfaces using modern materials that the industry has put to good use. Whether the horse world likes it or not the technological environment can and does affect it.

Internet communication

The internet revolution has finally taken hold in the equine industry, although only a small percentage of yards have taken full advantage of this advertising medium. Several websites list livery yards including the BHS website (www.bhs.org.uk) and all yards list contact phone numbers but very few currently have email or website links.

Competition venues and organisers have made better use of the medium, publishing details of clinics and competitions and allowing for entries to be made. Racing entries can be made online, with race goers able to buy entry tickets to racecourses. The Countryside Alliance (www.countryside-alliance.org) has made good use of the communication potential of the internet. Through mail shots such as the 'Grass Route', people in the industry are able to keep up to date with the key issues such as the ongoing hunting debate.

All weather surfaces

The all weather industry has made advances in recent years. The new surfaces are cheaper, easier to put down and last longer. This means that more yards are able to provide all weather arenas for their clients.

Veterinary medicine

The advances in veterinary medicine are good news for both horses and horse owners. However there is one down side and that is as treatments get more complex and expensive, insurance companies are forced to pay out more in settlements and this pushes up insurance premiums for horse owners.

LEGAL FACTORS

The legal environment is an extremely complicated and specific area, which is best handled by trained professionals. The importance of correct legal advice cannot be overstated and in any matters where as a business owner, employee or horse owner you think that there may be a legal implication, it is vital to seek immediate and accurate advice.

It is by its very nature directly attributable to the political environment because for any law to be passed, it must be approved by Parliament. It is therefore, to a certain extent, driven by the social and economic environments.

From a business perspective, the legal environment will cover not only legislation relating to equine matters, but all other aspects of life. These include financial, taxation, employment, health and safety, tenancies, land law, contracts and litigation issues. There is also the complication of European legislation such as the passport regulations and equine transport directives. The Department of Trade and Industry (DTI; www.dti.gov.uk) produces a guide to the regulatory requirements for businesses, together with a number of free publications. These are available from your local Business Link office (www.businesslink.gov.uk) or direct from the DTI.

An in-depth discussion of all the legal factors affecting a business environment is outside the scope of this book, however in the interest of providing examples we will take a closer look at a small number. For any of these issues, professional or legal advice should always be taken.

The structure of the business

One of the most important legislative issues that any business will face involves deciding what form the business will take. This important decision will have repercussions for every aspect of the business structure. The different forms of business are: sole trader; partnership; and limited company.

Sole trader

This refers to an individual who is self employed. The individual owns the business and all its assets and is entitled to earn all the profits. However, they are also responsible for all debts. Operating as a sole trader is a simple and flexible way of setting up a business. There is a requirement to inform the Inland Revenue, as taxation and national insurance will be payable on the basis of profits. Keeping accurate records is therefore not only an essential business function but it is a legal requirement.

Partnership

This refers to a business where there are two or more people who are self employed. It is recommended that there is a 'partnership agreement' setting out the shared areas of responsibility and ownership of assets. All partners are jointly and severally liable for all debts. There is a requirement to inform the Inland Revenue. Taxation and national insurance is based on the share of profits, together with each individual's personal financial situation, i.e. because two partners share profits equally does not mean they both pay the same tax. Problems can occur if a new partner wants to join, or an existing partner wants to leave, particularly over valuation. A partnership can be between individuals, or with a company.

Limited company

This refers to a business that is a separate legal entity. The company can be either a private or public limited company. Shareholders, who can also be directors, own the company. A director is not personally liable for debts, and a shareholder's liability is limited by the amount of shares owned. A limited company can be bought 'off the shelf', or created from scratch. All company registrations are handled through Companies House (www.companieshouse.org.uk), and there are strict rules and regulations associated with the set up of this type of company. There is the advantage of limited liability, but neither the shareholders nor the directors own the assets, as the company is the legal entity. As a director, you are employed by the company, and are not able to use the assets in the same way as the owner of a self-employed business. There is a higher degree of legal conformation required, which may be seen as onerous for a small business.

European passport legislation

The EU has issued a directive for compulsory registration of all equines and with effect from February 2005 it has become compulsory for all horses in the UK to have a passport. This stems from the fact that the horse is classified within EU law as a source of human food and it is therefore an offence to administer any drug for which no Minimum Residue Limit has been set.

The passport requires a section setting out whether the horse was intended for human consumption and, if so, to have any drugs administered recorded. It applies to all horses whether they were previously registered or not, including those kept for breeding and production. Each horse is be allocated an identification number and the documentation is intended to be similar to that already used for registered horses. If the horse is *not* intended for human consumption there is no restriction on the drugs administered.

> The Doyle report (April 2001) proposes a specific solution for horses because they are sporting and companion animals in the UK but food animals in the EU. It suggests that identification of horses by passport, and strict recording of medicine use, will allow horses to benefit from their unique treatments, while ensuring consumer health is not jeopardised (NOAH, 2001).

Contracts

A contract is a legally binding agreement between two or more parties. Contract law is considerably more complicated than many people realise and because of this it can be frighteningly easy for the unwary to get into difficulty. For this reason it is always advisable to seek professional advice when dealing with legal issues.

A contract does not need to be written in legal jargon or even signed or witnessed. The law of contract is designed to identify which agreements are legally binding and which are not. For a contract to be deemed valid there are several elements that must be present:

- There must be an offer on the part of the buyer and acceptance by the seller.
- The agreement between the parties must be made with the intention of creating a legal relationship.
- Each party must have the legal capacity to make the contract.
- The consent of each party must be genuine; it cannot be obtained under duress.

- The object of the contract must be legal.
- Each party must be in a position to uphold their side of the agreement.
- Consideration must be present. This means that there must be an exchange of money, goods or services.

If all these factors are not present then the contract will be deemed to be void, voidable or unenforceable. However, if all the above are present then in the eyes of the law a contract exists.

The time at which almost all horse people will be exposed to contract law is when they are buying or selling a horse, and there has been a variety of court cases that have arisen from this situation. The law of contract is also part of loan agreements, livery agreements, stallion nominations, employment contracts and a whole host of other agreements. Because this point of law can have far reaching implications and a wide range of complications, it is strongly recommended that if you are in any doubt, seek legal advice.

Health and safety

It is important to check your legal responsibility for health and safety of employees and the public and to register your business with the Health and Safety Executive or your local authority. You also need to investigate the requirements for a Fire Certificate. When you have five or more employees, you must have a Health and Safety Policy Document. This shows who does what, when and how.

The responsibility for producing the document lies with the employer regardless of whether you are self-employed, a partner or a managing director. Tasks can be delegated, but everyone must be aware of their specific tasks and you are still responsible to see that the tasks are performed adequately and that the member of staff is suitable and competent. The document covers employee consultation, usage of machinery and equipment, Control of Substances Hazardous to Health Regulations (HSE, 2002), display of information, training, accidents and first aid, working conditions, emergency procedures and risk assessment.

The Health and Safety at Work Etc. Act 1974 (see www.hse.gov.uk) is the main piece of legislation under which nearly all other regulations are made. Employers have a legal duty under this Act to ensure, so far as is reasonably practicable, the health, safety and welfare at work of the people for whom they are responsible and the people who may be affected by the work they do. People at work also have a duty under the Act to take reasonable care to avoid harm to themselves or others by their working practices and to cooperate in meeting statutory regulations. Other specific legislation may be applicable in the case of manual workers, new and expectant mothers, thermal comfort, ergonomic problems, noise levels and chemical usage.

Taxation

An in-depth analysis of the taxation law applicable in the UK is outside the scope of this book. However all businesses will need to be aware of the requirements from the Inland Revenue, whether they are self employed or an employer. An employer is responsible for deducting tax and national insurance under the PAYE (Pay As You Earn) system for employees and paying this over to the Inland Revenue. Self-employed people are responsible for their own tax and national insurance. A limited company is further responsible for paying tax known as corporation tax, on its profits. Information is available on income tax, national insurance and corporation tax, with regard to application and current rates (www.inlandrevenue.gov.uk).

Some businesses will need to consider their position as regards value added tax (VAT) and importing or exporting goods. VAT is a tax that businesses charge when they supply their goods in the UK or Isle of Man. It also applies to some goods and services from inside and outside the EU. VAT currently has three rates: standard, fuel and zero; however, some goods and services are exempt and have no VAT charged on them. If you are in business and your turnover (or sales), not profits, goes over the current registration limit then you must become VAT registered. This will mean charging VAT on your goods or services, and being able to recover the VAT paid on purchases. Current information is available from HM Customs and Excise (www.hmce.gov.uk).

It is important to be aware of these requirements and to discuss them and the implications for your business with a business adviser or accountant, as they will impact on your cashflow.

ENVIRONMENTAL FACTORS

Any activity that takes place in the countryside is guaranteed to have an immediate environmental impact. It therefore follows that the environmental factors will have an equally immediate impact on the activity. Many of the factors that could be considered in this section are also present in the sections already covered.

Regulations governing muckheap and carcass disposal are legal in origin although they have been brought about by environmental concerns. National Park, AONB (area of outstanding natural beauty) and SSSI (site of special scientific interest) status are often politically enforced because of social attitudes to the environment. It is up to the individual business to decide which issues are of specific relevance to their area of operation and in what context they wish to examine each issue. Further information on this type of issue is likely to be obtained from your local authority.

5 The competitive environment

Close examination of the external environment is vital if a business is to understand what is going on in the outside world but the analysis must not stop there. If an enterprise is to flourish it must pay close attention to its competitive environment. The term 'competitive environment' when used in a business context means any area that requires the business to compete, be it for customers, markets or supplies. By this we do not just mean competition from other businesses in the same field but also from other activities on which our current or potential customers might spend their time and money.

> The need to relate the business to its competitive environment is at the very heart of strategy formation (Porter, 1980).

The factors that make up the competitive environment are those that have a more immediate impact on the activities of the business than those considered in the PEST analysis. Although they are outside of its ultimate control the business does sometimes have the ability to influence them. It is up to the individual manager to understand which factors he can alter and which he is stuck with but, as with the external factors, the issues that arise still have to be dealt with.

The competitive environment can be seen as the interface between the external and internal environments, in other words it is the point where 'what we do' mixes with 'what everybody else does'. Because of the nature of competition it is easy for a business to think only in terms of the businesses offering a comparable service but this rather narrow-minded outlook can lead to problems. A riding school, for example, is competing for clients' time and money. It relies on customers choosing to ride instead of participating in another sport or watching their favourite team. This concept is one of the cornerstones to understanding the nature of competition in business.

As with the external environment analysis there are many different methods suggested in management textbooks. These academic
frameworks can seem rather abstract but by understanding the basic
mechanisms that are being applied and relating them to the equine
environment they will prove their worth.

FRAMEWORK FOR THE ANALYSIS

Because the competitive environment is a complicated and diverse area
it is again necessary to use some form of framework to structure the
analysis. Prolific business author Michael Porter devised the generally
accepted method. Porter's model of competitive analysis identifies five
forces in an organisation's environment that influence competition
(Fig. 5.1). These are the threat of new entrants, the bargaining power of
suppliers, the bargaining power of customers, the threat of substitute
products, and rivalry from competing firms.

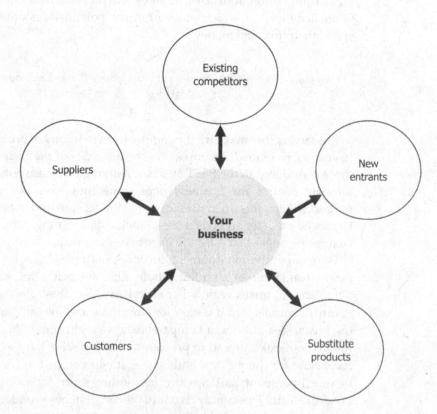

Figure 5.1   The competitive environment.

Porter (1980) took his lead from a field of economics known as industrial organisation and his model has much in common with the theories of perfect competition, oligopoly and monopoly used by economists to describe the competitive environment. These ideas are examined in more detail in microeconomic textbooks.

These factors need to be considered in turn but it is again vital to understand that they do not stand in isolation. As well as influencing and being affected by each other, they are also related to the external factors already considered and the business environment that will be examined next. It is important to always keep the context of the examination at the front of your mind because a new perspective on an issue that has already been considered may well throw up an important insight.

Porter's model does not claim to be perfect; it assumes that the industry itself is in a stable state and that only the immediate competitive environment for a specific business is being considered. It is not a business cure all, but used wisely it can help the manager to understand the competitive situations that the business finds itself in.

RIVALRY FROM EXISTING COMPETITORS

Although in the broadest terms a business is in competition with any and every other business that wants to part its customers from their hard earned cash, this particular analytical tool is only useful if the examination is more specific, i.e. it concentrates only on the most immediate competitive environment.

Porter (1980) maintains that rivalry exists when competitive businesses either see an opportunity to improve their position or feel the pressure from others.

Even the most well-established and successful business is constantly exposed to elements of competition from its rivals. This pressure can take several forms; pricing, levels of service and advertising.

Competition on price occurs when a rival business tries to entice away your customers by offering a comparable service at a reduced price. This is the basis of the business strategy known as 'cost leadership' and will be covered in more detail in Chapter 8. This type of strategy can lead to price wars but beware: if prices are lowered without fully considering the business's own cost structure then you could well end up with lots of customers who are actually costing you money.

By offering something that you can't, your rivals can try to poach your customers. This can take the form of a facility such as an indoor arena or a service such as clipping and plaiting. This concept is the key to the business buzzword 'product differentiation' and is covered in both the 'strategy' and 'marketing' chapters of this book.

Advertising can take many forms, be it a word of mouth endorsement, postcards in the local feed merchant or tack shop or a major media campaign. Major advertising campaigns are rare in small equine businesses but this does not mean that this type of competition can be ignored. However your competitors go about raising their profile, they have one aim in mind: to persuade your clients that they are better or cheaper than you.

THREAT OF NEW ENTRANTS

Before a new business can start up it will have to overcome a number of hurdles; these are known in business terminology as *barriers to entry*. These, combined with the way in which existing businesses retaliate to newcomers, will affect how attractive an industry is.

Barriers to entry are largely an economic concept. They include economies of scale, capital requirements, access to distribution channels, legislation and operational costs (Johnson and Scholes, 1997).

In order for an existing business to assess the threat there are a series of questions that need to be answered.

The first question to ask is 'What resources do they need to enter the market?' The level of resources required by a potential entrant to the industry will dramatically affect the ease with which new businesses can enter the market. Most equine businesses require a significant amount of time and/or money to be spent before they can start up. For example a farrier needs relatively few physical resources but must invest four years of his/her life in an apprenticeship whereas a livery yard owner needs no formal qualifications but must have a significant amount of capital tied up in buildings and land.

The second question to be considered is 'How attractive is the market?' The cost of setting up a new business, together with potential returns, will affect the number of people being attracted to the market.

The internet revolution initially generated hundreds of dot.com companies because the resources needed were minimal but the potential gains were huge. However the lack of performance of many of them subsequently affected the attractiveness to new entrants. In the equine industry the uncertainty surrounding the hunting ban coupled with the investment needed to start up made hunter liveries an unattractive new business venture in the early 21st century. This is a good example of the interaction between the external and the competitive environments.

The third question is 'What will they bring to the market?' This question is concerned with both capacity and differentiation. The capacity may take the form of extra stables or more horses shod whereas differentiation is concerned with the range of products and services supplied. In the livery industry, as has been discussed in Chapter 3, the issue of capacity has two levels: the first is the threat of new yards starting up; and the second is the threat of new horse places in private yards. The issue of differentiation relates to the variety of services offered to the clients.

BARGAINING POWER OF SUPPLIERS

The business's relationship with its suppliers is another important factor. These suppliers are able to put pressure on the business in a number of ways but the amount of actual influence they have will depends on their relationship with their own competitors.

By raising his prices a feed merchant can increase your costs but he runs the risk of losing you as a customer if there is another supplier that you can deal with instead. In order for the feed merchant to really apply pressure he must come to an understanding with his immediate competitors; this is known as collusion. The majority of small businesses will tend to deal with small suppliers so there is less danger of this occurring because most of the suppliers will be operating within what economists call perfect competition. This means that the suppliers can wield a very limited amount of power.

BARGAINING POWER OF CUSTOMERS

Customers can exert pressure by negotiating for lower prices and pushing for higher levels of service. By gossiping and comparing notes on services received they can effectively play one business against another. However, horse owners do not generally have the motivation to work together and exert group power because they tend to be a fairly disparate collection of individuals.

This bargaining leverage becomes more obvious when looking at the customer/client relationship that exists between two separate businesses. While the supplier may not feel the pressure exerted by one individual private client, it should be much more aware of the volume of business generated by a larger account holder. Although it goes without saying that a business should value every single client, human nature dictates that the ones who spend the most with you will have more influence.

THREAT OF SUBSTITUTE PRODUCTS

Porter's final competitive force is the pressure from substitutes. For the purposes of this analysis a substitute is taken to be an alternative product that can do the same job, such as margarine as an alternative to butter.

Because of the nature of the horse as an animal there are few real substitutes within the equine industry. For example, horses that are in work have to live in stables or paddocks and that really is the bottom line. Horses cannot live in kennels or housing estates or cow stalls so the only option to a livery space is for the owner to purchase their own land. It is beyond the financial scope of most livery clients to do this and many would not want to even if they could.

There are, however, some equine businesses that do have to be aware of the threat of substitutes; a manufacturer of horse boxes must be aware that he faces competition from not only other manufacturers but also from people selling trailers and towing vehicles.

6 The resource appraisal

It is all very well knowing the external factors that affect the business in every detail but unless the business understands its own environment in as much detail it will never be able to devise a suitable strategy for dealing with these factors. As has already been explained a small equine business does not necessarily need to go down the route of endless analysis and counter analysis but it is necessary to fully understand the inner workings of the individual business so that its ability to cope with these impacts can be accurately assessed.

In order to make the best use of the available resources a manager must have a complete understanding of all the assets that are at his or her disposal. When discussing business resources it is very easy to think only of the physical things but it is important to take into account the other factors that are working within the internal environment.

It is impossible for a business to make any sensible plans for the future without a comprehensive understanding of all the resources that are available. This means examining all the factors that make up the business, be they human, financial or intangible assets such as reputation, as well as the more obvious bricks and mortar.

The relevant factors will still need to be considered on an individual business level in order to accurately assess where the business is strongest and also where it needs to make improvements. It is essential to remain focused on the identity of the business that is being appraised in order to ensure that the analysis remains relevant. What may be an asset for one business could easily be a liability for another.

In order to get the most out of the resource appraisal it is important to remain focused on what the business actually does without being too narrow-minded. This means taking an honest look at the available assets while staying aware of what else they could be used for. A resource that is being underused or that is not suitable or appropriate can quickly become a liability.

When analysing the internal assets and workings of your own business it can be very difficult to remain objective. In some situations it may be useful to bring in outside expertise in order to arrive at an honest and realistic assessment of the business as a whole. It is, however, important to remember that any outsider will be hard pressed to gain an in-depth knowledge of every aspect of the business. For this reason the manager should be prepared to take a mixture of both his or her assessment and those of the adviser in order to see the complete picture.

SWOT ANALYSIS

The SWOT analysis provides another framework for the examination of the business environment. It allows both the internal and external environment to be critically analysed from a positive and negative point of view under the headings of strengths, weaknesses, opportunities and threats.

The SWOT analysis is suited to the analysis of a small business because it allows every aspect of the business to be examined within one framework. The disadvantage of this is that it can lead to a narrow field of assessment. However, like the PEST analysis it is not a faultless system. It needs to be carefully prioritised in order to stop strong threats and weak opportunities appearing to balance each other out.

> The SWOT analysis is considered by many to be the most useful management tool (Mercer, 1996) and in many ways it combines the five forces analysis with the PEST. The strengths and weaknesses cover areas already examined by Porter and the opportunities and threats look at the macro environment covered by PEST.

As with the other methods of analysis, while the SWOT analysis is a very useful method of identifying issues, it is advisable to then go on to examine the key areas of interest in more detail and to review these areas on a regular basis to ensure they are up to date.

The internal environment

The strengths and weaknesses in the analysis are the positive and negative parts of the internal environment. This part of the analysis includes, but is not limited to, the resource appraisal; it requires the business to look critically and honestly at its assets and their use. In some situations it may be useful to bring in outside expertise because it can be difficult to be objective from the inside. Part of the appraisal includes carrying out a risk assessment to comply with the Health and Safety at Work Etc. Act 1974.

The external environment

The opportunities and threats in the analysis are the positive and negative parts of the external environment. This part of the analysis requires the business to look critically at the external factors affecting its performance. This section of the analysis covers the areas already discussed under the five forces model and the PEST analysis.

Being aware of the areas in which the business has strengths, weaknesses, opportunities or threats, gives the manager the ability to make the most of events which may happen, enabling him or her to make the most of strengths and opportunities and overcome threats and weaknesses. If there is no awareness, this will not happen. The manager is able to use the information collected to help make decisions.

Because the SWOT analysis is not just limited to the internal environment, it can sometimes cause the analyst to lose focus. For this reason it may be useful to carry out a more detailed resource appraisal first.

RESOURCE APPRAISAL

Every business has a wide variety of resources at its disposal and it would be impossible to produce a comprehensive list on which to base a resource appraisal. It is, however, possible to divide these factors into five basic groups; these then form the skeleton for the more detailed analysis. These groups are:

- Equine.
- Physical.
- Human.
- Financial.
- Intangible.

The individual resources within each group then need to be considered with regard to both their benefit and hindrance to the business. Risk assessment must also be carried out for each group.

Equine resources

That the horse in itself is a valuable resource to most equine businesses goes without saying. It is the main source of income to a riding school and a competition rider. There are, however, several other, less obvious aspects to this resource that warrant mentioning.

The horse as a sponsorship tool

- Where the horse is a key factor within the business, for example a competition yard, it needs to be assessed with regards to not only its capital value, but also its value as an advertisement or marketing tool for the business.

- Many non-equine businesses are also in the position of having a horse as an asset, usually as part of a sponsorship agreement. In this situation the horse will be considered on its merits as a promotional tool, not just on its abilities as an animal. This can lead to communication problems between the interested parties.

The horse as a breeding resource

- A stud farm wishing to further the reputation of its resident stallions will need to assess the suitability of potential mares with regard to the standard of their progeny. Stallions are a major source of income on most studs and it is important that this investment is protected, and a clear policy is set out on the type of mare which will be accepted.

- Having horses as a resource on a stud farm also raises financial implications, particularly with regard to their valuation. The Inland Revenue has agreed a formula with the TBA, based on nominal value, not actual cost.

- A stud farm has some tax concessions with regard to business rates. The horse is classified as agricultural animal for the purposes of grazing and until it is broken, but not for the purposes of planning. For inheritance tax (IHT) purposes, buildings and land used directly for a breeding activity should qualify for IHT relief. There are also issues for capital gains tax. This is a complicated area of taxation and specialist advice should be obtained.

Physical resources

Physical resources are those which are easy to quantify. They are the fabric from which the business is built. Each individual asset needs to be assessed from the point of view of its current use as well as any potential uses.

The resources that should be examined in this group include, but are not limited to, those listed here. When compiling your own list it is vital to consider every facet of your business and consider each asset in context. It may also be useful not only to have a list of resources required in the future, to help with planning and budgeting, but also to consider each resource in terms of both current use and any alternative use; this will assist in identifying costs, revenues and benefits of each resource.

Land

Because of the nature of the horse as an animal, land is considered to be the key asset to many equine businesses. But 'land' does not just mean grazing; there are many more factors that need to be considered than just the quality of the grass. These include the following:

- The acreage available is an obvious issue for any business that involves keeping horses such as a livery yard or a stud. 'Acreage' does not just mean grazing, it also covers car park space, which is an issue for any business with visiting clients such as veterinary clinics, and tack and feed shops, space for storage, buildings and exercising. The available space is also of prime importance to any business with expansion plans.

- Every business has to address the problem of access. This can be a particularly difficult issue for businesses that must accommodate horse transport because of the size and manoeuvrability of lorries and trailers. Because of the regulations imposed by the Highways Authority there may be limits to the changes that can be made to the existing access and signing. Because of this, easy access to the road network and clear directional signs are a valuable resource. Good access is not just a matter of good lines of sight but also gate width, user-friendliness of any gates and the weather resilience of the surface. With the unhelpful nature of the British climate these last two are of particular importance to competition venues.

- The soil type has an obvious impact on any grass-based business. Good grazing is of prime importance to the majority of horse owners so well drained, fertile soil is a valuable asset to the business. The soil may also contain hidden assets such as copper and trace elements which are vital to equine health and can be expensive to supplement. Well drained paddocks are less likely to turn into the type of mud baths that can lead to mud fever and cracked heels.

- Grass quality changes in response to various stimuli such as grazing pressure, type of stock, date of mowing, drainage, nutrient status, introduction of weed seeds, pasture renovation and reseeding operations (Lockhart and Wiseman, 1993).

- Fencing needs to be well maintained and horse friendly. Fencing that can injure horses or allow them to stray is a liability which can result in legal and emotional upset. Stone walls and hedges, while making excellent field boundaries if well maintained, can be expensive to keep up because of the specialist skills involved; however, some areas can be eligible for grant aid.

- It is essential to identify the utilities both available and required. This includes electricity, water and telephone.

Buildings

The design and construction of any buildings is another important factor in assessing the potential of the business, particularly when considering any expansion plans. When carrying out the assessment it is important to consider, amongst other things, ventilation, size, aesthetic appeal, safety, access and security.

The buildings need to be considered in respect of state of repair and cost of maintenance as well as looking at other potential uses, the optimum use and the opportunity cost of all the possibilities. This examination should not just be confined to the buildings currently being utilised but should include all buildings available to the business. Even derelict stone barns may have a value as reclaimed stone and tiles.

When assessing the conversion potential of any currently utilised buildings it is important to consider the cost of any necessary alterations, particularly the addition of services such as drainage, water and electricity.

Machinery and equipment

When assessing this resource it is important to consider all the equipment used by the business. This means taking an inventory of everything from clippers to horse transport. The available equipment and machinery need to be considered in respect of financial value, utilisation and usefulness.

Specialist pieces of equipment can be expensive to purchase and maintain and are often not essential to the running of the business. The value of this type of equipment should be assessed in terms of the labour saving and convenience factors. Although quad bikes and horse walkers represent a significant investment to many businesses they can have a huge impact on the staff, both in their attitude to their work and their efficiency.

Some machinery, such as chain saws and sprayers, can also involve additional costs in the form of training courses for staff and also have health and safety implications. These extras, although not always obvious at first sight, all contribute to the running costs. In situations like this what appears to be an asset may in fact be a liability because it may well work out cheaper and more convenient to bring in an outside contractor.

> The National Proficiency Test Council starts a week's foundation course at £250 for basic chainsaw handling. The next step is intro-felling at £300. Safety gear is required to be tested and labelled.

Within a veterinary practice, there is little point investing in a £10 000 scanner if the number of clients potentially requiring its use is very small. Assuming that the scanner has an asset life of 4 years, then if a fee of £50 is charged per scan, a minimum of 50 scans per year would be required just to recoup the capital cost. A useful analysis tool would be to look at how many clients in the last year have been referred to other practices, because a scanner was not available. Alternative solutions would need to be compared to ensure that the practice was not wasting its investment. (This would include other capital purchases within the practice using the same money – the opportunity cost of choosing one asset over another.)

Make the most of vehicles used within the business. For example a horsebox, or a farrier's van is not only vital for transport but is also a valuable method of advertising. Use signage to give the business name and contact information. Look at getting local companies to sponsor their own advertising on your vehicle and generate a contribution towards the maintenance costs. It is important to assess the suitability of a vehicle, as a six-horse lorry only used for four horses could be a liability. It would require an HGV licence, so less people can drive it, it would be more expensive to run, be difficult to park and take up space etc.

Facilities

The business needs to pay attention to all the facilities it has at its disposal. Like the buildings, the facilities need to be assessed in terms of state of repair and cost of maintenance as well as looking at other potential uses.

A business needs to ensure it has the appropriate facilities both to attract and keep clients. For example a livery yard geared towards the recreational rider may provide facilities geared towards enjoyment and safety. A yard aiming to attract competition clients would, however, have to pay more attention to the facilities necessary to prepare horses for competition such as horse walkers, arenas and gallops.

Facilities such as all weather surfaces and coffee rooms may not be considered essential to the running of the business but they are good selling points and so need to be considered with respect to both state of repair and the cost of maintenance.

If a farmer is reviewing his facilities and thinking of diversifying it is worth noting that new set ups under diversification effectively qualify for full business rate relief for five years, they get 50% from government and a discretionary 50% from the local authority. However, diversification does require planning permission!

Human resources

The skills and abilities of both the management and staff need to be assessed with regard to all characteristics. As has been mentioned under the social environment of the PEST analysis, good staff are becoming harder to find and keep so it is important to ensure that they are regularly appraised, rewarded for their efforts and receive recognition when due.

It is necessary to identify what is required within the business by each member of staff, to communicate these requirements and to evaluate on a regular basis. This will ensure that a suitable training and development plan is produced and provide a way of rewarding the staff when appropriate.

It should be remembered that motivation for staff will not just include their monetary recompense, but will also include their benefits. It should be remembered that 'conditions' under which staff work also include the atmosphere created within the workplace, by fellow colleagues as well as management. Bullying or lack of respect can lead individuals to feel demotivated and no amount of financial recompense will suffice. This applies both ways! Other conditions within an equine business can include accommodation and hours worked. It has long been taken for granted that staff living on site are available 24/7 and this should not be the case.

When appraising members of staff, it is worth taking into account their attitude, their flexibility, their ability to build and maintain relationships (with other staff, management and clients), as well as recording their expectations in terms of job satisfaction. A member of staff who proves particularly adept at handling conflict could prove to be worth their weight in gold!

Financial resources

The financial stability of the business is obviously a key factor. The availability of extra capital for expansion plans or weathering difficult times needs to be considered as do the terms of any existing loans. This information will need to be looked at in conjunction with the information gathered in the economic section of the PEST analyses because the loan and credit terms will be tied to interest rates. All these factors need to be considered on an individual business level in order to accurately assess where the yard is strongest and also where it needs to make improvements. This type of analysis is of no value unless it is carried out honestly and realistically.

All businesses need to have capital. For the majority, this will mean borrowing money. In order to decide how much, from whom and over what period, it helps to look at the alternatives available:

- Generous relative or friend: this may be the cheapest option but is not generally available to all. If it is available, then the repayment terms should still be agreed in writing to avoid later disputes.

- Bank loan: this can be in the form of a fixed or variable loan. The rates of interest and the repayment method can be tailored to suit the item being purchased. Costs should be built into projections so that different repayment schedules can be compared, prior to making a decision regarding purchase. If the potential purchase will generate revenue, then projections should show how long the item will take to pay for itself.

- Bank overdraft: this type of finance should only be looked at as a short-term solution and should be agreed in advance to prevent unnecessary charges. Any potential needs should be identified through the cashflow projections. It is useful to know potential times during the trading of a business when an overdraft may be required – how much and for how long – so that costs of financing an overdraft can be compared to other forms of finance such as short term loans. Businesses such as trekking centres, which are busiest potentially during the summer, may need to arrange overdraft facilities during the early part of the season when feed and bedding need to be bought in advance. An alternative may be to discuss credit terms with the supplier.

- Mortgage: as a source of finance this is used primarily for the purchase of property and is available through a variety of institutions.

- Grants: the availability of grants should be investigated to determine whether or not a business qualifies for this support. Make the most of DEFRA, Business Link agencies and other rural business support which may be available.

- Sponsorship: this is often a source of finance where the company offering the sponsorship will benefit in some way from using the equine business as a vehicle for promoting its own. Make the most of the skills and abilities that you have within your business to offer a unique service to other companies. These can be related to your own business, for example feed merchants or clothing companies, or may be seemingly unrelated companies such as solicitors, accountants or electrical suppliers.

- Other: leasing is used for financing vehicles and equipment but ownership is not transferred at the end of the agreement. Hire purchase may be used to finance the purchase of vehicles or equipment, with ownership transferring at the end of agreement. An asset bought in this way is treated as an asset of the company, with the interest and charges being an allowable cost.

Intangible factors

Yard reputation

Although this is not a tangible factor it is, nevertheless, an important part of the business. It can take many years for a yard to gain a good reputation but in an industry where most recommendations are by word of mouth it is a very important asset.

Presentation

Appearance of staff and facilities can greatly enhance or ruin a business reputation. Vehicles should be clean; staff should be neat and tidy, appropriately dressed for the work they do. All clients should treated with respect and in a polite manner.

Customers

A solid client base is vitally important for a strong business. It is all very well attracting new customers but unless you are in the position to keep your existing customers happy your business cannot grow. The best advert for any business is a satisfied customer. The predicted value of sales to the existing client base is often given a financial value in the sale of a business and in this way is translated directly into a financial resource shown in the balance sheet as goodwill.

Relationship with suppliers

A good relationship with the suppliers of a business can make the manager's life significantly easier and is therefore worth cultivating. It can manifest itself in discounts, prompt service and favourable payment terms. For the large corporate business these terms may be granted due to volume of business but for the smaller company these benefits are more often than not due to the relationship formed between the people involved.

Risk assessment and control

The Health and Safety Executive defines a hazard as anything that could potentially cause harm and a risk as the likelihood of that hazard's potential being realised. A risk occurs when a hazard and people come together. In assessing risk, the severity and likelihood need to be identified, together with the main ways of reducing this. Not all hazards are immediately recognisable and differ in the sort of harm that they can cause.

Some hazards result in injury, others in ill health and some can result in both. For example, incorrect lifting can result in both injury to the back and ill health caused by the muscle damage. Exposure to stress is more likely to cause ill health rather than immediate injury.

Risk assessment and control is central to safety management – that is, the ability of the organisation to provide an environment which has been assessed with regard to level of risk relevant to the hazards that are present.

To appraise the number and levels of hazards within an organisation requires an in-depth inventory to be undertaken. This should be combined with the appraisal of each category of resource, observing the practices of clients, suppliers and employees together with the physical layout of the premises, tools and equipment used. These observations should be recorded and monitored.

Each hazard identified then requires a 'rating' in terms of Likelihood and Severity to give a final Risk Factor. The Likelihood rating could be on a scale of 1–5 with 1 being very unlikely and 5 being almost certain. The Severity rating could range from 1 for an injury needing only simple first aid to 5 being a fatality or disabling injury. This is *before* any workplace precautions are implemented.

In the case of a stud farm, a hazard could be identified as 'Covering a mare'. This hazard has a likelihood of 5 (it is after all what happens on a stud!) and a severity of 4 (being a potentially dangerous task). This gives a final Risk Factor of 20 (5 × 4). The workplace precautions that can be implemented to reduce or minimise this risk are covered in the next chapter.

This may seem a harsh assessment; however, consistency is the key to carrying out a realistic assessment of risk within a particular environment. To carry out the initial 'potential risk' requires the assessor to look at the environment with 'fresh' eyes. It can be related to perception and may require more than one viewpoint, as each person will see a different set of hazards.

With regard to our resources that have been appraised, the suggested areas for assessment are as follows:

Equine

- Differences in handling stallions, mares or mares with foals at foot and youngstock.
- Turning out or bringing in procedures.
- Leading horses mounted or unmounted.
- Teasing, covering and other specific stud work.
- Attendance of the farrier or vet.
- Restraining horses.
- Suitability and capability of work being performed.
- Mucking out and general stable duties.
- Loading horses for transportation.
- Feeding.

Physical

- Using machinery such as horse walker, yard blower, tractor, steam cleaner, clippers, school harrow.

- Lifting and carrying feed bags or buckets.
- Manual work such as tack cleaning, using tools, forks, brushes or hosepipes.
- Using medicines and chemicals, such as creams and ointments or weed killer and pesticides.
- Electricity.
- Rubbish and obstructions.
- Zoonoses such as ringworm, leptospirosis or salmonellosis.
- Other risks such as tetanus and dust.

Human

- Untrained staff.
- Suitability of tools and equipment.
- Computer usage.
- Allergies.
- Suitability of clothing.

Financial

- Security of cash.
- Fraud.
- Theft.
- Loss of records.
- Confidentiality.
- Computer systems.

Intangible

- Reputation.
- Stress.

An organisation is required to show that it has not only assessed the hazards and risks, but that it has taken the appropriate steps and the necessary precautions to reduce or minimise these hazards and risks. The management of hazards and risks identified will be covered in the next chapter.

Part 2
Managing a Business

7 Resource management

Management of the resources available to a business is crucial to its survival and growth. However, it is important to distinguish between what is essential to the day-to-day operations of the business and what activities will contribute to efficient management but are not in themselves crucial to success. Without this distinction a lot of time and effort can be expended in areas which do not actually contribute to the core business.

In any business there is a list of tasks that are required on a daily basis and while it is patently obvious that a livery yard must muck out the horses every day, and a farrier must shoe horses, this is not what is meant by resource management. Resource management is those tasks which must be performed on a regular basis to ensure the efficient and effective continuation of the business.

In order to effectively manage your resources it is absolutely essential to keep up to date and accurate records of what has been done and when it needs to be done next. Without this basic information there is a real danger that essential maintenance will be missed and legal requirements omitted. There are also records that must be kept by law. We will look at the necessary records under each type of resource to identify those that are required.

EQUINE RESOURCES

There is a vast amount of literature and advice already available on the subject of how best to look after a horse. As this is not a stable management book but a business management book we will not be covering this subject in any detail. There are, however, a number of businesses within the equine industry that will have equine resources, and the management tasks that they must perform will relate to their business activities. For example the business management issues that relate to a stallion at stud are vastly different from those for a competition horse.

Equine records

It goes without saying that anyone keeping horses, whether as a rider, owner or service provider, needs to maintain accurate records for the horses in their care. These records should cover what has been done to each horse and what needs to be done in the future.

Historical records should include amongst other things worming regime, visits from farrier and vet, injuries and illness, visits from the equine physiotherapist and dentist, work done and competition performance. Planning records should cover the dates of vaccinations and other treatment, competition entry deadlines and fitness programmes.

This list is by no means exhaustive and will vary greatly depending on what business you are in and in what capacity you are caring for the horses. For example, a stud will need to keep more specialised records relating to mares and stallions.

PHYSICAL RESOURCES

When thinking about resource management the first type of resource that comes to most people's mind is the physical resource. The system of maintenance that is most commonly found in equine businesses is of the 'fix it when it is broken' method. By implementing a more structured approach to planning maintenance it is possible to save both money and time.

Some forms of maintenance, for example a vehicle's MOT, will have a predetermined and legally enforced timescale, so it is important for the business manager to recognise this in advance and adapt the business's activities accordingly. Other types of routine maintenance may be sensitive to time or weather conditions and so the maintenance schedule will need a degree of flexibility.

It is also important to recognise that many of these activities are carried out by other businesses and so forward planning is essential.

Land management

Because many yards do not have access to the relevant equipment the maintenance of the paddocks often falls to outside contractors. The fact that this sort of operation needs to be planned and booked well in advance is often complicated by the unpredictable and unhelpful nature of the British climate. Operations such as rolling and harrowing are best carried out when the ground is in a certain condition but this may not always be possible despite the manager's best efforts to plan ahead.

By ignoring the need for regular and effective paddock maintenance you run the risk of ending up with weed infested, horse sick paddocks with no nutritional value. These will then need a significant investment of time and money to put right. The neglect of car park areas can result in weeds and potholes, which are both unsightly and off-putting to clients and expensive to rectify.

Building management

Basic building maintenance such as clearing gutters and painting can often be carried out by the business's employees. However larger projects such as roof repairs may need to be carried out by specialist builders. The neglect of buildings can be incredibly costly, with what would have been a small repair turning into a major reconstruction. Insurance claims that result from self-imposed neglect may not be paid out.

It is also necessary to plan for any future building works, be they government imposed, such as improving access for the disabled, or scheduled improvements and alterations.

Vehicles and equipment

It goes without saying that the loss of a vehicle can have a major impact on the daily activities of a business. This is equally true of items such as computers and clippers. It makes sense to schedule the repair and maintenance of these items when they will be missed least. To send clippers to the repair shop in November is obviously not optimum resource utilisation. As has already been stated you will need to be both organised and flexible when you are relying on a third party to carry out work required.

There may well be a health and safety or insurance requirement to routinely service pieces of equipment, and any receipts or invoices for this work will need to be kept as evidence that the work has been carried out by an approved contractor.

Facilities

The facilities offered by a business can be a major incentive for their clients. It therefore follows that if these facilities are allowed to degenerate this will result in dissatisfied customers. Short-term maintenance, such as harrowing and pooh picking in an arena, can greatly extend its life.

By planning for all these operations in advance and advising both clients and service providers of your intentions and requirements you should be able to continue normal business activities with the minimum of disruption. You should also be able to gauge in advance the likely cost of the maintenance and work this into your financial planning.

HUMAN RESOURCES

One of the key resources within any business is the people involved. This does not just mean the staff, it also includes the clients. The issues involved in keeping these groups happy are very different but the required end result is identical in every case, for each person to feel satisfied.

Staff

Finding and keeping good staff, at all levels, is essential for any business. The subject of staff can cause employers many headaches, but those that take the time and effort to appreciate their staff, in more ways than purely financial, will reap the rewards in the long term. Being recognised as a 'good' employer makes it easier to attract and retain staff; this makes the investment in training and development a worthwhile action.

Similarly, staff committed to their employer should be rewarded. Staff who make the effort to attend on a timely basis, who are neat and presentable, who make the extra effort with clients, who show respect for the owner/manager are more likely to develop a mutually beneficial relationship with their employer and, should the need arise to change jobs, be highly recommended.

As a business grows it is important to recognise the changing requirements for level and number of staff. Although temporary staff can help out on a short-term basis, the recruitment of permanent staff does not happen overnight and it is important to remember that it will take time to train any new team members and that allowances must be made while the team adapts to the new structure.

Training and development

The provision of training and development is another incentive to keep staff motivated. Training while you are working is a good way of improving skills and well-trained professional staff reflect positively on the business. When planning staff training time it is important to make provisions for the inclusion of new members of the team.

The National Vocational Qualification (NVQ), together with the foundation and advanced apprenticeship system, are ways of training the staff while they work. They are assessed in the work place in the appropriate skills needed to carry out the job.

An employer should keep records of all staff training activities including induction courses and staff appraisals.

Staff appraisals

Staff appraisals are, in their most basic form, an opportunity for employers and employees to sit down and discuss matters of mutual concern. They are often used in larger corporations but very rarely seen in the horse world except in the form of a reprimand as soon as anything goes wrong. The subjects raised could include aspirations, performances and future plans for both parties. This type of discussion is important because it will make the employee feel valued and part of the team and it can help the employer develop future plans for the business. The appraisal can be carried out as an informal chat so long as the outcome is recorded.

Should there be cause for disciplinary measures it is important to remember that employees have rights and there are legal procedures that must be followed before they can be dismissed.

Employment records

An employer has a duty to keep records relating to its employees for all wages and salaries paid together with records regarding absence (sickness/holidays). This includes details relating to deductions from salary for taxation, national insurance, maternity pay and other benefits as required by law. Employers are required to make payments to the Inland Revenue and submit annual returns at the end of the tax year. For any business that requires help and advice, the local Inland Revenue office details can be found in the phone book. Each employee is entitled to receive a contract of employment setting out the terms and conditions under which they are employed. It is a legal requirement that an employer takes out employer's liability insurance and displays the certificate in a public place. As with any issues which involve a legal or financial implication, it is strongly recommended that professional advice be obtained.

Risk assessment

A risk assessment is an overview of the daily tasks that are likely to cause harm and injury to anyone who may be affected by the activities in the workplace, including contractors, i.e. vets, farriers, painters and so on. Every activity carries a risk in itself and it cannot always be removed so it is important to make clear in the policy document that the risks have been identified and that measures have been put in place to minimise and control these to ensure the safety of the employees.

It is therefore important that employees have an appreciation of risk and do not create or ignore any hazards. Staff should be able to identify and deal with risk in the appropriate manner by identifying which can be dealt with safely and which should be reported to the appropriate person. Risks can be reduced by training staff in, for example, how to operate machinery, how to deal with horses, how to handle chemicals and medicines, by keeping machinery serviced and used correctly and by making protective clothing available when needed and ensuring staff make use of these items. They should undergo an induction training, having all the procedures explained and being shown how the equipment is operated safely.

Risk assessments should be updated and reviewed on an ongoing basis. Should the control measures not be working, if there is a change in the activity or situation, should the people change or if there is a change to the current legislation then the document will need updating.

Clients

A business is dependent on its clients, as without clients there is no business. It is worth looking at how you keep your client records, to ensure they are simple but effective in assisting you to run your business. Accurate client records will help if you wish to carry out a mail shot, or use the details to send out questionnaires. Up to date contact records will be needed in order to carry out 'after sales' service. However, you will need to be aware of the data protection laws if you intend to keep information about your clients on a computer.

FINANCIAL RESOURCES

Financial transactions

Keeping records of all financial transactions is not only a legal requirement but also a fundamental necessity to allow planning and decision making within the business. A basic requirement is to keep records of income (money coming in) and expenses (money going out) together with all supporting evidence.

Sales/income

Keep copies of all invoices raised and a record of all cash sales if a proper till is not available. Monitor payment of invoices and chase regularly for outstanding items. The presentation of your invoices can say a lot about your business, so make sure they are clear and simple, but contain all relevant information.

Purchases/expenses

Keep all invoices paid. It can be useful to mark the cheque number or method of payment. Different filing methods can be used, i.e. by supplier or in payment order depending on how you may wish to access the information subsequently. Monitoring levels of expenditure by supplier can help with negotiating discount or credit terms and may also be useful if you are seeking to secure sponsorship.

Bank account

Keep an accurate record and make a note of the reason why a payment was made using cheques, standing orders and direct debits. Also keep a record of all receipts banked. Keep chequebook stubs, paying in books and statements. Negotiate with your bank to obtain the best terms regarding charges and facilities. Do not be afraid to question items on the statements.

Petty cash

Cash is used for smaller items but must be strictly controlled. Keep a set float (e.g. £50) and keep all receipts.

Income and expenditure account

An income and expenditure account (or profit and loss statement) can only be produced in an accurate and timely manner if the above records are kept. It reflects a summary of the total income and expenses for the business and for tax purposes is usually prepared once a year. A detailed analysis of tax allowable expenses is outside the scope of this book and professional advice should be obtained. If accounts are produced more frequently then they can provide a useful tool for analysing the performance of the business. They may be produced in slightly different formats, depending on their use. They may then be referred to as 'management' accounts.

Balance sheet

A balance sheet is a statement prepared at a given point in time to show the position of the business in terms of its assets and liabilities. Again it is usually produced on an annual basis; however, it must be remembered that the position can change rapidly. The size of your business will determine whether the balance sheet will contain a lot of detail, or be very concise. Figures given in the balance sheet can be used to give an indication of the stability of the business.

Budgets

Preparing a budget allows an owner or manager to plan the activities of the business, understand when events will happen and what effect they may have on the profitability of the business. It should not be assumed that costs and revenue would always go up month on month or year on year; the advantage of preparing a 'new' budget each year is that individual items can be reviewed and amended as necessary.

Projects

It may be useful to prepare a budget when applying for additional finance, or for original finance at the start-up of a business. It is then possible to see trends in income and costs that can indicate where additional revenue needs to be generated, or costs need to be saved. Being aware of at what point a business becomes profitable, the break-even point, can help in planning for taking on additional resources. Any necessary capital expenditure can be planned for, showing whether a loan is required. One-off projects can be prepared with their own budget, showing whether they produce a profit or not. As registration for value added tax (VAT) is required at a given sales level, a budget will allow this point in time to be identified, and a decision taken as to whether this is in the interests of the business or not.

Performance

Using a previously prepared budget to compare to actual performance can be a useful monitoring tool; this does not just apply to financial budgets but also to resources in general, particularly when horses are involved. Reviewing a budget is an ongoing process, not a one-off event! Estimating revenue and costs can be a difficult process at the start, but can be refined with additional knowledge.

Partial budget

Individual budgets can be prepared at any time, for example when pricing a new service or deciding whether to take on a new venture. When used in this way, as a management tool, they are called 'partial budgets'.

Cash flow

It is important for a business to know what levels of cash are moving in and out of the business. Cash flow is not just about level of sales, as a sale may take months before a customer pays you. Nor is it about level of expenses as you may take months to pay your suppliers. It is about when money comes in and goes out. A cash flow is an extension of the budget process in that it helps a business budget for cash movement.

A cash flow forecast should show what money is coming into and out of the business, when it comes in and out, why it is happening and when it is happening. This then identifies where there may be a surplus or a shortfall and whether there is the opportunity to earn interest on deposit or be prepared to pay interest for an overdraft facility.

RISK ASSESSMENT

Having identified the hazards and risks within an organisation as part of the resource appraisal, there is a requirement to deal with them. This entails either removing the hazard, avoiding the hazard or putting in place suitable precautions to minimise the risk. Which course of action is to be taken depends on whether it is reasonable, practical or cost efficient.

It is, however, not enough to do this as a one-off process. To allow an organisation to monitor and evaluate the hazards and risks identified, there should be a risk control system. This can be set up as:

- Identify the main hazard.
- Carry out a risk rating (Likelihood × Severity).
- Suggest workplace precautions.
- Adopt suggested precautions.
- Calculate risk reduction resulting from the implementation of these precautions.
- Record, monitor and review on a regular basis.

In our example from the previous chapter of 'Covering a mare', it is neither reasonable nor practical to remove the activity from the organisation. The management process therefore is to suggest and adopt the precautions required:

- Training of staff in the correct procedures and communication methods.
- Correct restraint by using a bridle, of both the stallion and the mare.
- Wearing protective clothing such as gloves, hard hats and steel toecap boots.
- Usage of non-slip floor coverings.
- Using an enclosed area.
- Restriction of access to essential staff only.
- Protective boots for the mare.
- Examination by vet to ensure mare is covered at optimal time.

These precautions when implemented would then lead to a reduction in risk factor from 20 (5×4) to 6 (3×2). This reflects that there is still a 'likely' occurrence with regards to likelihood but only a minor injury resulting from any possible incidents. Any incidents occurring would be recorded within the accident book, allowing management to review the procedures on an ongoing basis.

As part of the review process it is necessary for management within an organisation to regularly communicate any changes in legislation or procedures that have been identified. This communication should be two-way; as well as giving staff information, management should be prepared to listen to suggestions from staff perhaps via a nominated representative or safety committee.

When reviewing or implementing precautions it is useful to identify answers to the following questions:

- Who is responsible?
- For what are they responsible?
- When should the work be done?
- What is the expected result or output?

These questions should ideally be answered at the planning stage, but are useful to ask throughout the review and monitoring process. When the expected results are documented, it is easier to monitor actual performance against expected performance.

It is important for an organisation to include the current risk assessment procedures within the induction process for new members of staff, as well as communicating changes to existing staff. As part of this process it is essential to identify any training needs to ensure that staff are able to comply with the precautions in place to minimise the risks associated with their role.

8 Strategic planning

Any source of business advice, be it a book, a consultant or an MBA course, will tell you that all businesses from sole traders to global conglomerates need to have a strategy. Following a good, distinctive strategy should ensure that a business builds, maintains and continually strengthens a specific identity in the market place.

> So what is a strategy? There are numerous definitions available.
> It can be described as a plan, direction, or guide for a course
> of action. Put simply it is a pathway to get from where the
> business is now to where it wants to be in the future
> (Mintzberg et al., 1998).

Many equine businesses are of the opinion that they need a business strategy in the same way that a fish needs a bicycle. However, it is worth considering that very few people would even go shopping without an idea of where they were going, how they intended to get there and what they wanted to buy, yet they have no qualms about having no firm plans for their business.

Although strategy has been the darling of business analysts for the last 30 years its origins go back much further. The idea of employing a strategy has been around for centuries but it has been the area of expertise of generals and military leaders rather than businessmen and academics. One of the most important recorded doctrines in military strategy originated in China at around 400 BC and was written by Sun Tzu. These ideas were then further developed by Clausewitz in his book *On War*. Both of these documents are referred to in the vast majority of contemporary strategy literature.

So how can the analyses of large scale warfare help with the successful running of a small equine enterprise? The often unique nature of the equine industry can lead to difficulties in relating the situations it faces to the current ideas of the business strategy community. It can be helpful to go back to 'first principles' and look at the original thoughts that the current crop of ideas is based on. It is then possible to develop a strategy that is more appropriate to the problems in hand without having to disassemble the interpretations of others first.

In order to succeed in battle or business it is important to have a clear idea of where you are planning to get to. Without a clearly defined or closely followed strategy companies and armies of all sizes tend to lose sight of their direction when they hit difficult times.

ASSESSING THE SITUATION

Before deciding on a course of action it is important to gather and analyse as much information about your own situation as well as that of the competition. It is for this reason that the environmental analysis examined in the previous three chapters is so important.

> Tzu understood that it is not enough to fully understand your own position and devoted much attention to the importance of being informed about the position and strength and attitude of the enemy. He said: 'Know your enemy and know yourself and you can fight a hundred battles without disaster' (Tzu, 1971).

The value of accurate, up to date information cannot be over stated. A rider would not plan a competition season without carefully examining the competition schedule and assessing the capabilities of the horse. It follows that the same amount of fact finding should be applied to business planning. Without a clear understanding of the issues being faced by yourself and your competition it is impossible to make any reasoned decisions about your future plans.

Once the facts have been assembled it is up to the management to process the information in a manner appropriate to the situations being faced. It can sometimes be helpful to discuss the wealth of sometimes contradictory information with an outside expert because it can be very difficult to be completely objective about something as important to you as your own business. Even top riders will consult with trainers about the performance and preparation of their horses because, as everyone knows, the person on the ground can get a very different view from the person on top.

There are many problems faced by managers trying to understand and cope with their environment. They need to be aware that their interpretation of these issues will relate to and be affected by their own personal perspective (Johnson and Scholes, 1997).

SETTING TARGETS

It is rare in the equine industry, particularly the service sector, to find a business that has either a mission statement or a set of objectives. It is therefore very difficult for the managers to judge how their business is developing. When implementing a new plan it is important to have some method of charting the progress of the business in order to ascertain whether or not the plan is succeeding.

Most businesses will have several aims relating to different sections of the business and different times in the business life cycle. In order to achieve these sometimes contradictory objectives it may be necessary to accept a trade-off between targets. It is important to remember that many aspects of business, despite the best efforts of analysts, are unpredictable and the changeable nature of some decisions will have implications for the strategy that the business employs.

The mission statement

The British Olympic Association mission statement is: 'To develop and protect the Olympic movement in Great Britain in accordance with the Olympic Charter' (www.olympics.org.uk/thisistheboa).

Although it is vital for the business to have a clear idea of where it wants to get to, this 'idea' on its own does not constitute a strategy.

'Little Farm Equestrian Centre aims to provide a superior livery service for competitive dressage clients. The centre intends to achieve and maintain a reputation for excellence in the training and production of dressage horses and riders.'

This statement on its own, although it clearly sets out how the business wants to be perceived and which market it is targeting, is not a strategy. It is a mission statement. From this statement alone it would be very hard to determine how well the business is performing because there are no measurable achievements or timeframes set out.

While a mission statement is invaluable in a corporate environment because it is a clear and concise method of communicating to both employees and clients what the organisation is aiming for it is not so essential in a small business where communication networks are smaller and theoretically simpler.

The objectives

Although the mission statement has great value as a statement of intent it needs to be quantified. This is where objectives come into the equation but there is more to devising objectives than just assembling a wish list. In order to be of any use as a management tool the objectives set must be quantifiable, concise, realistic and consistent. It is also important to think carefully about the time scale being considered, e.g. long, medium and short term objectives. The objectives can be applied to several areas within the business: performance; finances; and physical objectives.

> Mercer (1996) notes that it is vital to have a clear aim and time scale in mind in order to steer the business along the correct path. Forming objectives is the key to the entire process. Although Mercer specifically applies this statement to the marketing process it is equally true for strategy formation.

Performance objectives

Whatever strategy is being pursued the aim is almost always to maximise resource utilisation. Or in equine terminology to fill as many stables, or shoe as many horses, as possible. The percentage occupancy of the yard is a clear and easy way to interpret measurement of performance. The client turnover is another useful gauge for success. A good yard tends to have a low turnover so a high turnover is a reliable sign that something is probably not going to plan. A competition or racing yard could also set targets for competitive achievement such as winning a certain amount of money or upgrading a set number of horses.

Financial objectives

The financial objectives for a business can be quite simple. Because the business's finances are at the very heart of the plan it makes sense for the objectives to be financial in nature. They could be approached from either a costs or profits angle but need to be clear, concise and quantifiable. The financial objectives could be goalposts in their own right or could be linked to the funding of improvements to the yard.

Physical objectives

The yard could also use further improvements as objectives, for example increasing the number of stables or adding more facilities to ensure that the yard stays ahead of the competition.

When setting objectives it is sensible to give serious thought to what is and is not realistically achievable. To set goals that are too easily accomplished is no challenge whereas impossible goals can be disheartening. It is also useful for the business to bear in mind that the objectives can be set up over a variable time frame and need not all be achieved in a short time. A good strategy should have a reasonable shelf life so that the business can continue to grow. With this in mind it is important to review the objectives on a regular basis in order to make sure that they remain relevant.

DEVISING THE STRATEGY

Having decided that the business needs a strategy and assessed the external and internal factors that will affect the business in the future, it is time to start making plans. The mission statement and objectives are the obvious starting points but a strategy must be more than just a series of objectives. It must take account of all available assets, acknowledge the strengths and actions of competitors and be both flexible and strong.

> A good example of the difference between an objective and a strategy can be borrowed from popular fiction. In *The Lord of the Rings*, by JRR Tolkien, whilst Frodo only had an objective Gandalf had a strategy.

There is no shortage of literature available on the subject of business strategy and it all discusses the important facts and issues but many of the books tackle the subject from a corporate perspective. This means that it can be very difficult for an equine business manager to scale down the issues covered and untangle the relevant bits of advice. This does not mean that the information and advice is of no value to the equine business, it just means that a little lateral thought needs to be applied to the issues.

In reality the strategy document drawn up for a small business is likely to be a series of objectives linked by a methodology. It is not necessary to draw up a complicated, step-by-step guide to world domination if you are realistically aiming to increase productivity by 5% and gain a foothold in a new area. This theory holds true for both business and military situations; in the same way that a large corporation's strategy document would be much more complicated than a small livery yard's, the battle plan for a tribal conflict would be on an entirely different scale from the Duke of Wellington's plans to rid Europe of Napoleon.

MILITARY THEORIES

The military origins of strategy theory and the analogy that this allows has not been lost on strategy authors and there is a wealth of literature that explores the comparisons. As has already been mentioned Sun Tzu's original ideas are still relevant today and form the starting point for most of the contemporary analysis. Tzu was the first to fully explain the importance of a complete knowledge of both the internal and external environment. He broke warfare down into its component parts in order to more fully explain the importance of each element. The art of war, he maintained, is governed by five constant factors:

- The moral law: what drives the people to follow their rulers regardless of the risks. In business terms it is the human dimension that causes employees to trust and follow the directions of the boss.

- Heaven: the intangible factors that affect the plan – night and day, cold and heat, times and seasons. These all play a part in business decisions in the modern world, particularly night and day; in the global economy it is very important to consider time zones.

- Earth: the physical factors such as distances and geography. In today's context it means examining the more tangible factors and how they can affect the outcome.

- The commander: the virtues of wisdom, sincerity, benevolence, courage and strictness.

- Method and discipline: the organisation of the army – subdivisions within groups, the hierarchy among the officers, methods of controlling the army and maintenance of the supply chain. In more modern terminology it is the logistics side of the strategy, the 'how' part of the plan.

This original treatise was then developed further by Prussian soldier and writer Carl Von Clausewitz. He developed his ideas during his service first in the Rhine campaign as a young soldier and throughout his career, which ended as the director of the Berlin Military Academy. His ideas were influenced by the campaign and battle tactics of Napoleon, who was waging war across Europe for much of Clausewitz's service years. He is best known for his observation that war is just a continuation of politics. Of the modern 'business warriors' Denis Laurie is one of the most prolific. In his texts he draws heavily on both historical and modern military campaigns. He compares the tactics and strategies employed by military leaders with those used in business situations.

> Clausewitz (1968) notes the rarity of truly accurate information. He states that the greater part of information in war is contradictory, a still greater part is false and by far the greatest part is of doubtful character. What is required of the decision maker is the discrimination which comes from knowledge and good judgement.

Laurie (2001) states that there are 10 basic strategic options employed in both war and business: attack strength; attack weakness; strategy of change; concentration of forces; forming a strategic alliance; patience and time; control the choke point; relentless attack; containment; and combat readiness. Although the implementation of the strategy will vary from situation to situation the intended results are remarkably consistent: whether you are involved in a battle or a business deal, the objective is always victory.

> The ability of software giant Microsoft to compete at all levels is due to a strategy of 'combat readiness' reminiscent of the strategy employed by special forces units such as the American Delta Force and Navy Seals. Bill Gates himself is quoted as saying of his business operation: 'We are talking about life and death in every piece of e-mail' (Laurie, 2001).

The comparison between military and business strategy is so popular with business analysts because the analogy works in almost all business situations. By comparing the resources and circumstances within the business environment to those found in battlefield situations the strategist is able to visualise the problems being faced and 'play out' various options.

PORTER'S GENERIC STRATEGIES

The most commonly quoted strategy theory has been developed by the American academic Michael Porter. Although the actual strategies employed by organisations can be as varied as the organisations themselves, Porter maintains that this infinite number of options can be condensed down into three basic ideas: overall cost leadership; differentiation; and focus. From this he has developed what is known as Porter's Generic Strategies. He states that in order for a strategy to be successful it must be followed in isolation. He believes that a business which does not focus completely on one game plan is in danger of becoming stuck in the middle and failing to reach any of its targets.

Cost leadership

The aim of the cost leadership strategy is to become the lowest cost producer in the industry. This can be achieved in a number of ways including monitoring costs, taking advantage of economies of scale and improving production facilities. The cost leadership strategy is the strategy that most yards would like to think they have, but without suitable monitoring systems in place and a better than average equine accounting system it is doomed to failure. For a business to follow a successful cost leadership strategy it has to have some method of generating a financial advantage over its competitors. This can be achieved in any number of ways but usually involves either lowering business expenses or better utilisation of resources.

This type of strategy will suit a yard offering a basic service that does not have access to any outstanding features that it can use in its favour, such as a highly skilled head groom or a purpose built arena. Not every business is in a position to practise a cost leadership strategy. A business that is paying a large monthly rent is already at a big disadvantage over one that owns its own facilities. This gives an immediate advantage to farm diversification projects and private yards with spare stables where the facilities are existing, under-used resources that do not represent a significant cost to the enterprise. A farm diversification scheme, which has access to a ready supply of straw and hay produced at home at cost price, is ideally suited to implementing a cost leadership strategy. This type of enterprise, offering a basic DIY stable rental service with no expertise provided and no additional facilities, is in a position to offer a comparable service to its competitors' at a slightly lower cost to the client while still maintaining a larger profit margin.

Once the cost of the service has been calculated it is then necessary to do some market research and ascertain how much is being charged in nearby yards so that the weekly charge can be set. The yard will then have to be careful to monitor the actual cost of providing the service to ensure that profit margins are maintained as well as keeping tabs on competitors' prices in order to maintain its position in the market. As has already been explained it is vitally important to continue to monitor both your own and your competitors' progress.

Differentiation

Differentiation involves the development of unique products and services. The business aims to stand out from the competitors by being better or faster and relies on brand and customer loyalty to maintain its position. For a business to follow a successful differentiation strategy it has to have some method of generating a physical or intangible advantage over its competitors. This can be achieved either by offering a level of service or facilities over and above that provided by other businesses in the vicinity.

This is the strategy that most yards, be they livery, competition or racing, are in a position to implement in one way or another. It involves the development of a service that in some way stands out from its competitors and then relies on creating customer loyalty to maintain this position. A yard which either has an existing feature that its competitors lack or has the capital to extend its facilities is well positioned to pursue a strategy of differentiation.

An equine veterinary practice that has diagnostic and treatment facilities on site is in a position to offer a more immediate service to clients than one which has to refer patients to a better equipped practice for further consultations. As equine clients become more informed and demanding, this level of service will give the practice a definite competitive edge over and above some of its rivals.

It is not just facilities that can be used as a selling point but also the skills of the staff and management. As such it can offer a perceived value to the client over and above that offered by the cheaper yard and can therefore justify its higher charges. A business with a good management structure and efficient, knowledgeable staff can also differentiate the service it offers by tailoring it to the client's requirements. This strategy can bring increased benefits to the clients as well as improving the profit margin without excessive financial investment. It costs nothing to ask the clients what they require and the improvements can often be implemented with a minimum of fuss but a vast increase in goodwill and customer satisfaction.

The focus strategy

A business which concentrates its service on a narrow and specific segment of the market has a focus strategy. It involves the development of a service that in every way is geared towards a particular type of horse or owner. In order to successfully focus on a particular group of clients everyone within the business must have a clear understanding of the requirements of their clients. This type of strategy is often unconsciously implemented by the simple expedient of 'like attracting like'. For example a manager with a particular interest in eventing will often attract fellow eventers to the business simply because they move in the same circles. For a business to follow a successful focus strategy it has to have a very clear idea of what its target client needs and wants. This type of service is often more expensive and so while offering potentially higher profits also involves more demanding clients.

A yard which already has a key area of interest is ideally situated to focus its business on that area of the market. If a manager is involved in a particular equine discipline it is likely that he or she will have a good understanding of its particular demands. It is also likely that he or she will already have contacts, both potential clients and services, in the discipline in question. Focusing on a particular discipline does not just depend on know-how but also on facilities. Each discipline requires a different training method and this requires a specific range of equipment. The provision of these facilities can be costly and a yard will need to be absolutely certain that the demand is there before making a significant investment. A yard which intends to target competition riders will need to provide adequate areas for parking lorries and trailers. Storage for expensive tack will also be essential and this will need above average security arrangements. It will also be necessary to provide clipping and washing down areas with adequate water supplies and lighting.

The three competitive disciplines are not the only groups of riders who have specific needs and it is not just the higher end of the market that can be focused on. A yard in an area with particularly good hacking, such as the New Forest in Hampshire, can design its service specifically for hackers and pleasure riders.

A yard situated in a prime hunting area, such as the Beaufort hunt country, is ideally situated to focus on hunter liveries. Hunter livery is both labour and resource intensive. The yard must be prepared to provide a groom with the ability to drive a lorry and know the way around the hunting area. The groom must also be able to prepare horses fit and smart enough to hunt. This requires both riding and grooming skills as well as specialist equipment such as clippers. This is one of the most common focus strategies in the livery industry.

A farrier can also make use of his or her specialist skills by focusing on a particular service such as shoeing racehorses or remedial farriery. The additional skills necessary for both these specific activities lend themselves to a focus strategy.

The service should be consistent on all levels and the management needs to constantly remind itself that its customers are likely to have a clear aim in mind for their horses and will be expecting assistance in achieving these aims. By targeting a narrow and specific client base the management leaves itself little or no room to manoeuvre should it hit a problem. If for any reason the client base dries up the management will have to do some very fast thinking if it is not to be left in an impossible situation. This can be graphically illustrated by the problems being faced by the hunter livery sector at the moment. If the current political threat to hunting is realised there are a large number of yards whose primary source of income will dry up overnight.

ASSESSING THE OPTIONS

Very rarely will a business find itself in a position where there is only one way forward; it is therefore necessary to examine the options open and then make a decision. Once a strategy has been implemented it can be very difficult to change direction so it is vitally important to make the right choice before you start utilising resources and directing funds.

Rumelt (cited in Mintzberg et al., 1998) suggests a framework for evaluating the available options. Each possible strategy is subjected to a series of questions in order to assess whether or not it is suitable for the individual business. These questions are:

- Consistency: Does the strategy present mutually compatible goals or are there any built-in irreconcilable differences?
- Consonance: Does the strategy present a flexible response to the external environment?
- Advantage: Will the strategy provide a competitive advantage for the business?
- Feasibility: Is it possible to implement the strategy without over stretching resources?

Whilst this framework provides a series of logical and practical steps, it fails to consider the most important factor in small or family business decision making. The strategy with the best chance of success will not always be implemented because it may not be acceptable to the people making the decisions. It is important to never underestimate the human factor. If a strategy does not fit in with the organisation's identity and self-image it is unlikely to succeed.

Handy (1995) examines the different styles of management and organisation that grow up around different personality types. He notes that the culture of any organisation is both a product of and the guidelines for the collective attitudes of the workforce.

With this in mind a more suitable framework for assessing the options open to a small equine business could consist of just three questions: 'Is the solution suitable, feasible and acceptable?'

Suitability

The suitability of a strategy is dependent on the current activities of the business. Does the new idea fit in with what is currently occurring? This is not yet concerned with logistics or morals but more with the strategic logic and relative merits of the different options. This acts as a screening process before embarking on the more detailed analysis of 'Can we do it?' and 'Should we do it?' (Johnson and Scholes, 1997).

Feasibility

The question of feasibility is concerned with whether the organisation has access to the physical and mental resources required to execute the strategy. It is a waste of time to devise a strategy where the number of horses in the yard doubles over the next five years if there is no way that the physical capacity of the yard can be expanded because of planning restrictions. This area of assessment relates closely to the resource appraisals done as part of the SWOT and PEST analyses. It must also look to the future, 'If we don't have it at the moment can we reasonably expect to get it in the near future?' This can be difficult to assess because it can relate to financial and mental expansion, not only 'Can we afford to do it?' but 'Are we capable of learning how to do it?'

Acceptability

The question of acceptability in a small business, particularly an equine small business, can be very complicated. Whether or not the people within the business will tolerate the changes that need to be made can be impossible to assess. Individuals can have very conflicting ideas about 'the type of business we are' and 'the type of people we do business with' which can lead to heated arguments and stalemate.

The self-image of a business is an intangible concept that is inextricably linked with the culture of the organisation. It is the attitudes, ideals, beliefs, motivations and thoughts of the people that make up the organisation. This 'shared idea' is reflected in the traditions, habits and symbols of the business and its environment, particularly where the industry as a whole is as steeped in tradition as the equine environment. This is due in no small measure to the part that the horse has played in our history as a nation. The 'Three Day Event' competition originated as a training exercise for cavalrymen and modern day equestrian skills still relate back to the use of horses in warfare. The horse world has always been resistant to change, it seems to be the very embodiment of the phrase 'if it ain't broke don't fix it' and this can be seen in every aspect of the industry.

> Maslow's hierarchy of needs sets out the intangible factors that individuals will be fighting for: physiological security, actual security, social well being and ego. This includes the prestige and size of their departments, their pay packets and those of the workers in their departments, their job security, their personal gratification and social standing (Maslow, cited in Johns, 1973).

In order to try to understand the culture within an organisation it is important to find out how that culture evolved. In order to understand the 'why' of the present it is necessary to get to grips with the 'because' of the past. This means delving into the history of the organisation and the people.

The people within the group will inevitably have their own prejudices and preconceptions that make up their personal opinions.

All these idiosyncrasies and agendas can mean that the obvious solution to a problem may not be implemented because it just wouldn't seem right to the people involved. To a consultant this will be intensely frustrating but there is little point in fighting it because where emotions are involved logic can and will be ignored. This is true of even the most experienced strategists. For example, throughout his successful career the Duke of Wellington was biased against night attacks. While campaigning in India as a young commanding officer he was involved in a failed night attack. This defeat stayed with him for the rest of his military career and resulted in a deeply held prejudice against night fighting (Cornwell, 1998).

IMPLEMENTATION

The best strategy in the world is of no consequence if it is not effectively implemented. This may seem like a simple matter of following the plan but this is not always the case. The business environment has much in common with the battlefield in that the various elements that influence it are constantly changing. In order to be successful a strategy must be both focused and flexible.

The SWOT and PEST analyses are important as they not only pinpoint the current location of the business but also serve to flag up any future problems. As has been mentioned already there are no end of interpretations of the reasons behind the defeat of Napoleon at the battle of Waterloo. Even the Duke of Wellington himself famously stated that it was a 'near run thing' (Roberts, 2002). One of the more commonly voiced opinions is that Napoleon was so fixed on the strategy that had won for him on so many other occasions, the 'concentration of forces' strategy described by Clausewitz (1968) and Laurie (2001), that he failed to either notice or respond to the changing circumstances around him:

> 'Even if you're on the right track you will get run over if you just sit there.' (Rogers, cited in McCormick, 2001).

With the benefit of hindsight it is easy to see that not all strategies work out as they were first intended. Many emerge as the situation unfolds around them and this is not a bad thing (Mintzberg *et al.*, 1998). It could be said that the important thing is to remain focused on the ideas and objectives behind the strategy without becoming entangled in the step-by-step logistics. A strategy is, after all, a guideline for progress but not a rigid prescription. In the horse world in particular it is important to remember that the horse is an unpredictable animal in its own right and cannot be relied on to abide by any plans its owner may have.

Once the strategy has been put in place it is important to implement some form of control in order to check the progress of the business. This means a system built into the strategy that can tell the management whether the correct path is being followed and also if it is still leading in the right direction. This would be considerably more difficult in a larger business because the lines of communication are longer and more complex.

The action plan

The detailed action plan should be a clear and concise set of instructions covering what will be done, when, by whom and how much it is likely to cost (Kotler, 2002). It needs to be understood by all the relevant parties and integrated into their own plans. There are several other key points that need to be covered:

- At what point should existing clients be brought into the discussions? It will be necessary to discuss any imminent changes with the existing liveries before the changes are made in order to avoid the misunderstandings and disagreements that are likely to happen if the current clients feel that their views are not important to the management.

- Ordering equipment. If the plan involves purchasing equipment to fit in with the new colour scheme or bearing the business logo it will be necessary to order it well enough in advance so that the suppliers can organise quantities or alterations. It makes sense to implement this part of any plan outside the competition season so that any changes are in place ready to start the new season.

- Individual responsibilities. If any plan is to be smoothly and efficiently implemented it is important that everybody involved knows what their responsibilities are and is clear on how and when they are to be implemented.

The methods of control

Clear controls should be built into the plan to allow the management to gauge the progress on a regular basis. It is no good discovering that you are six months behind at the end of the year because by then it is too late to rectify the situation. Control measures can be temporal, financial or, in the horse world particularly, based on competitive achievement.

- Temporal controls are easy to define but not always easy to stick to. Time limits and deadlines are sometimes rendered unattainable by circumstances beyond the control of the company such as supply problems. It is important for the management to recognise factors beyond their control and remain flexible. For example aiming to build an arena in six months may seem to be perfectly feasible but if the suppliers have a four month waiting list and the area in question is flooded for a further three months the objective cannot physically be met.

- The financial benchmarks set by a business should be realistic. Like the timescales, they need to be clear and concise. It is important to monitor the financial goals set by the plan because at the end of the day most businesses' prime concern is making money. Raising profit margins by a set amount or cutting costs by a percentage are measurable objectives but still need to be grounded in some timescale. It means nothing unless the 'by when' is also clearly stated.

- When dealing with horses one of the best gauges of success is competitive achievement. Competitive achievements as goals are a good way of gauging the progress of a yard because they can be clearly charted. Competition results are regularly published so the business can gauge not only its progress but that of its competitors as well. This gives another useful benchmark for the management team to compare with its rivals.

9 Marketing

The concept of marketing is one of the most misunderstood and underestimated in the equine business world. Although the thoroughbred breeding and retail sectors of the equine industry have a good grasp of marketing practice there is a significant number of business managers within the industry whose marketing strategy begins and ends with an advert at the local saddlers, as and when they need to drum up some more business. This state of affairs demonstrates a complete lack of understanding for what marketing actually is. It is much more than advertising; it is nothing more or less than the way in which the business presents itself to the world.

Marketing definitions often include the use of business jargon such as 'creating demand', 'adding value', 'facilitating customer satisfaction' and 'dynamic relationship' when in fact it is simply finding out what the customer wants, then persuading them that you have got it!

> Mercer (1996) suggests that modern marketing theory really came about as part of the rise of advertising in the 1950s but that it was not until the 1960s, with the rise in product differentiation and consumer preference, that it settled into its current form.

Marketing has much in common with business strategy in that there is no end of conflicting advice available on how to go about it. In fact the only thing that everyone seems to agree on is that it is vital to carry out some form of marketing strategy if a business is to survive in a competitive market place. Like strategy, marketing as an academic discipline is a relatively new concept. In practice marketing has been part of human existence since the first tribe started bartering with its neighbours but it was not until the industrial revolution that the ideas behind the modern marketing theories started to emerge.

Marketing in the equine industry, aside from the racing and breeding sectors, tends to be restricted to the retail and manufacturing sector.

However, as competition amongst the livery sector strengthens it is likely to become increasingly important for yards to create a good first impression amongst potential clients and this is all part of the marketing process. There is no 'one theory' that can be applied to every situation but there are several 'rules of thumb' that can be used to provide a more flexible framework on which to base a strategy.

Marketing theory is far from an exact science. It goes much further than just placing adverts or making sales; these are just the end points of a process that begins even before the individual product takes shape. More than any other business function, it deals with the needs and desires of the customer.

> Kotler and Armstrong (2001) suggest a simple definition of marketing as being: 'the delivery of customer satisfaction at a profit'.

Every time a business interacts with a customer, or potential customer, it is participating in the process of marketing. Every time you deal with a customer, be it face to face, by e-mail or even just passing them on the road, you are in a position to alter the customer's perception of your business. This is marketing at its most basic level.

MARKET ANALYSIS

In order to succeed a business needs to have a clear understanding of the environment it operates in so that it can attract new customers and keep existing customers happy. It is essential for the business to understand not only what its customers actually want but also what its competitors are capable of supplying. Market analysis is therefore an integral part of the marketing process.

Market analysis is not just a duplicate of the analysis carried out as part of the strategy formation. It is specifically looking at the factors that impact on the end product's ability to deliver customer satisfaction. The competitive environment analysis already carried out examines many of these areas but it is not good enough to just re-name these results and try to superimpose them on the marketing environment. Competitive environment analysis examines factors on a 'whole business' level. The marketing analysis needs to concentrate on the specific interaction between the business and customers, so the issues covered will be central to this relationship rather than the more general 'them and us' type of issue already covered. While it is, of course, possible to look at these areas as part of the competitive environment it is vital to be able to focus on the purpose of the research. To retain clarity of thought it would be best in many situations to carry out a separate and specific marketing analysis.

> Marketing can be defined as: 'Activities that facilitate and expedite satisfying exchange relationships in a dynamic environment through the creation, distribution, promotion and pricing of goods, services and ideas' (Dibb et al., 2001).

When analysing a market it is very important to get a feel for not only the way things are now but also the historical reasons for this state of affairs. It is important to understand the internal workings of the market in order to effectively understand the factors affecting demand and therefore predict as accurately as possible the actual demand for the product. It will also help to decide the optimum placement of the product in the short and long term. It is important to focus on the object of the analysis, marketing strategy, in order to avoid merely repeating the earlier analysis and drawing no new benefit.

MARKET RESEARCH

When most people think about market research, they picture an under-paid, lonely individual with a clipboard harassing shoppers outside a supermarket. Although this is part of the process, it is not the whole story. Market research involves finding out as much as you possibly can about the particular market you are aiming for. It is often carried out as part of the development of a new product but just because nobody else makes something does not necessarily mean that there is a gap in the market, and it is advisable before spending time and money developing your unique idea to make sure there is a market in the gap. Nobody has yet developed beer flavoured horse food, but just because the product does not exist does not mean that it is a product waiting to be manufactured; it means nobody wants it!

Some of the methods of analysis already used in the business environment research can be refocused for the purposes of researching the market. The PEST analysis is no exception:

- The political issues that are specifically relevant to the marketing plan include the effects on industry of consumer pressure groups and the environmental lobby groups.

- Economic issues are central to marketing theory because markets require purchasing power and people and the available purchasing power in an economy depends on income, the availability of credit and levels of savings, so these factors are very important to marketers.

- Although social trends are not easily overturned they can change considerably over a number of years. This can be illustrated by the change in the attitude towards fox hunting in the UK. The British Field Sports Society became the Countryside Alliance in 1997. This evolution occurred with the changing political role that the society was required to fill. Its mission statement is 'To campaign for the countryside, country sports and the rural way of life'. It is important to acknowledge the amount of influence that the media can have over the attitudes of the general public.

- The information revolution that has arisen from the use of the Internet has also started to have a marked impact on social trends. The technological revolution has had both a direct and lateral effect on the external environment and this provides a good example of how the different factors can affect more than one area of influence. Internet purchasing has far-reaching implications for suppliers and could well change the shape of buying and selling in years to come.

THE MARKETING MIX

The most commonly used framework for analysing the marketing environment is the marketing mix or four Ps. This method was championed by Kotler (2002) and concentrates on the main factors relevant to the marketing of the enterprise: Price, Product, Place and Promotion (Fig. 9.1). As the service industry has developed, the marketing mix has had to evolve to cope with the factors specific to the marketing of a non-physical product. This has resulted in the inclusion of People, Process and Physical evidence.

These factors are all controllable variables because they can be changed by the business, but only within the constraints that are imposed by the external and competitive boundaries. It is up to the individual business to develop a marketing mix that suits its needs and purpose.

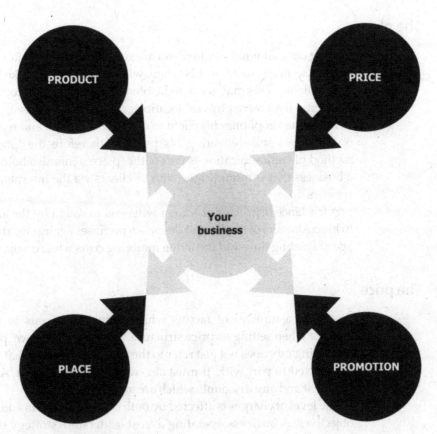

Figure 9.1 The marketing mix.

The product

It is important for a business to identify 'what' its product is; this is not as simple or obvious as it first seems. The 'product' is not just the actual service or physical good that is produced, it also includes the package, the branding, the warranty, the delivery and customer service that the end consumer receives. It is a known and accepted fact in the advertising world that the best advert in the world cannot sell a bad product, so it therefore follows that it is very important to make sure that every aspect of the product is right.

The product for a vet is more than just a cured horse, it is a satisfied owner who has received a confident and correct diagnosis from a calm and knowledgeable veterinary surgeon, as well as a horse that has recovered with the aid of a trained professional.

The place

Having defined what product you are supplying, the next key question a business needs to answer is when, where and how to make the product available. This may seem to be obvious, but there is much more to the 'place' than mere physical location.

When the vet phones his client to discuss the patient and reassure the owner, he is still delivering his product, therefore the 'phone' as a method of communication is part of the 'place'. This also holds true for a business that communicates with its clients via the Internet, as many retailers do.

A freelance instructor or trainer will need to weigh up the advantage to his customers of teaching at their own premises against the disadvantage of wasting time and incurring motoring costs while on the road.

The price

There are a number of factors which a business needs to take into account when setting its price structure. That said, the 'price' part of the marketing mix does not just refer to the amount of money that the client is expected to part with. It must also reflect terms of credit, method of payment and any discounts which are to be offered.

The level of charges is affected by both economic factors and strategic objectives. A business operating a 'cost leadership' strategy obviously needs to pitch its prices lower than its competitors, whereas a business operating a 'focus' strategy can charge a premium for providing a specifically tailored product.

The promotion

In any business situation it is not enough to just have a brilliant plan for the future. How are you going to attract customers if your target audience does not know about it? In a battle situation it is advantageous to keep your plans secret; in a business environment it is not so clever.

The 'promotion' element within the marketing mix relates to the communication about the product and the organisation. This can take the form of advertising campaigns and education and is essential for both new and established products.

By driving from yard to yard in a van with his name and contact details on the side, a farrier effectively promotes his business activities.

This method of promotion is also put to good effect by a large number of competitive riders and their sponsors using the side of horseboxes.

In an industry as vocal as this one, it is important to recognise the impact of word of mouth testimony from both satisfied and dissatisfied customers. It is a truism that while a happy client will tell three people, an unhappy client will tell anyone willing to listen!

Research has suggested that the majority of livery yards were recommended to their clients rather than attracting their attention by adverts. This serves to reinforce the point that the main form of communication within the industry is by word of mouth and the best advert for a yard is satisfied customers.

The people

The 'people' element of the marketing mix is the most variable because people can be both unpredictable and fickle. There is more to keeping clients happy than delivering a good product at a competitive price; often the key factor in customer satisfaction is the level of service provided by the staff. The best product in the world when delivered by surly and uncooperative employees will leave a bad impression, whereas friendly, efficient and sincere assistants can go a long way towards repairing the damage done by a less than satisfactory product. It is acknowledged within many successful restaurants that a customer with a complaint who is dealt with in a considerate and competent manner is actually more likely to return than one who just receives an excellent meal.

MARKETING STRATEGIES

The development of a marketing strategy is not just a simple matter of promoting a product but a multi-faceted process that can impact on the entire business. The majority of equine businesses have many areas and skills and can supply a range of services. This is particularly true of the livery sector. It can be difficult to apply some of the textbook strategy to what is, in effect, a very individual series of products or services. It would be impossible to devise a single marketing strategy which would apply to clipping horses and arena hire, but by looking at the bigger picture, the yard as a whole, it becomes easier to apply a logical framework to the process and achieve a cohesive strategy. This is why it is so important to carry out accurate market analysis before embarking on a strategy formation.

Porter split business strategy ideas into three categories; marketing strategies can be split into two.

Market segmentation

> Kotler (2002) uses a variation of the five forces model to examine the marketing environment but in his model the customers are in the very centre of the diagram. This reflects the fact that the centre of the marketing world is the customer whereas in a whole business strategy the customer is only one aspect of the environment.

Whatever business strategy a business pursues it is, to a certain extent, aiming its service at a specific segment of the market. It is therefore important to correctly identify who is being targeted and how to communicate with them. It is vital to realise that not all customers want the same thing.

Rather than trying to appeal to an entire cross section of a market, which may involve fighting with superior competitors and superior products, it is more realistic for a company to identify the parts of the market that it can serve most profitably and concentrate its forces on that area.

> 'You can please some of the people most of the time but you can't please all of the people all of the time' (attributed to Abraham Lincoln).

The major segmentation variables for consumer markets are geographic, demographic, psychographic and behavioural but there is no 'one right way' to segment a market. It is up to the business manager to find out what works best for his business and his industry.

> Kotler and Armstrong (2001) state that market segmentation is: 'dividing a market into distinct groups of buyers on the basis of needs, characteristics or behaviour who might require separate products or marketing mixes'.

Geographic segmentation

This involves dividing the market into areas such as nations, regions, counties, towns and neighbourhoods. This could also include riding club and pony club catchment areas.

Demographic segmentation

This involves dividing the market into groups based on human variables such as gender, age, marital status, occupation and education. Of the 2 million horse riders in the UK 33% are under the age of 15 and the ratio of female to male riders is 3 to 1 (BETA, 1999a, b).

Psychographic segmentation

This splits the market into groups according to attitudes, personality characteristics, social class and lifestyle. This could also include preference for competitive disciplines or breeds of horses.

Behavioural segmentation

This divides prospective clients into groups based on their knowledge, uses and response to the product.

Product differentiation

> The American Marketing Association (cited in Kotler, 2002) defines a brand as: 'a name, term, sign, symbol, or design or a combination of them intended to identify the goods or services of one seller or group of sellers and to differentiate them from those of their competitors'.

Product differentiation is the process by which a product or service is given a unique identity which distinguishes it from its rivals. This process is known as branding.

The concept of branding has become so universal that virtually everything from fruit to political parties has some form of brand identity. As consumers we have become familiar with 'Chiquita bananas', the Nike 'swoosh' and the Trakehner antlers.

The idea has come a long way from the 'brand' that ranchers used to stamp on to their cattle and horses.

Brand equity is the value of the brand based on the levels of customer loyalty, recognition and perceived quality that is attached to it. A strong brand equity is a very valuable asset to a company; the Coca-Cola brand is estimated to be worth in excess of £50 billion and Microsoft, £35 billion. A brand that is perceived to be powerful can give a company a better bargaining point when dealing with suppliers. It also allows the company scope to extend its range from under the protective umbrella of an already trusted name.

Branding is not an unknown concept in the horse world. Studs have been jealously guarding their prefixes for years and many breed societies will prevent a horse or pony from being registered with a prefix unless it has been bred by the stud concerned. By making sure that only the animals that are up to the expected standard are registered and sold on and making sure that the best examples are competing at high profile competitions, the breeders manage to make their names synonymous with quality and talent. This is the very essence of branding.

To be successful a brand needs to be consistent. Saddlers like Stubben and Pessoa have created a whole corporate image that clarifies their basic values. Their name on a product projects an impression of quality and good design.

Triple Olympic gold medallist Mark Todd has been very successful with his 'Mark Todd' saddles, rugs and equipment. Through attention to detail and clever marketing he has turned his already recognisable name into a high profile equine brand name.

THE MARKETING PLAN

A formal, written marketing plan is much more likely to be used by a large corporation than a small business. It provides a clear point of reference for the marketing activities of the business, and the planning process itself offers a valuable opportunity for productive discussions between the key personnel in the business.

The marketing plan as a whole document needs to be clear, concise and consistent if it is to be carried out effectively and achieve its aims for the business. It is probably the most important product of the marketing process. These qualities can just as easily be applied to the type of plan that would be of benefit to a farrier or a livery yard.

Within the corporate environment, marketing plans are becoming more customer and competitor orientated and planning has developed into a continuous process rather than a once a year occurrence. However, it is important to take full advantage of inputs and advice from all areas of the business because the marketing plan is not exclusive to the marketing department (Kotler, 2002). As the equine industry becomes more focused on business issues it will need to take these practices on board, but it is unrealistic to expect small businesses of any nature to have either the resources or budgets to warrant large-scale marketing departments. It is nevertheless important to realise that these ideas and practices can usefully be scaled down to suit the individual needs of a business.

There are a number of key areas that must be covered in a marketing plan:

- *The executive summary*: as with the strategy document or business plan it is important to set out, at the very beginning of the document, the basic facts contained within. This may take a paragraph or a page depending on the complexity of the report but either way it must be clear and concise.

- *The current marketing situation*: this section contains a brief run through of what the business is currently doing and whether or not it is working.

- *The opportunity and issue analysis*: this section contains an analysis of the issues relevant to the formation of a new marketing plan. It includes the results of the market research and the ideas developed within the marketing mix.

- *The objectives*: setting objectives is not just an important part of strategy formation, it is also the cornerstone to the marketing plan. As with the strategy formation, it is important to set objectives that can be easily measured. This means that they must be achievable and quantifiable. Saying that you want to expand the customer base is inadequate unless you add the 'by how much' and 'in what time frame' that pin down the definite aim.

- *Defining the marketing strategy*: having examined the relevant issues and defined where the business wishes to go, it should now be in a position to work out the marketing strategy that will best achieve its objectives. The strategy should be a programme which brings all the business's objectives together in one manageable plan of attack.

- *Action plan and control mechanisms*: this part of the document follows the same format as its counterpart in the strategic plan. It is vitally important for exactly the same reasons: unless everyone concerned knows who is supposed to do what and when, there is no chance of the plan being carried out with any degree of success.

The control mechanisms have been discussed already as part of the strategy document formation.

10 The business plan

A Business Plan can fulfil a number of roles. It can be an internal document that lays out the overall strategy and marketing plan for a business, an initial business start-up plan or a proposal for one-off projects. It can therefore be used as a 'selling' document or as a management tool. In each case the intended audience must be taken into account during the preparation. A good Business Plan needs to be realistic but should indicate that success is anticipated. It should include both short and long term considerations.

There are some general rules which should be borne in mind during the preparation process. These cover the layout, the purpose, the characteristics of the business, and in many cases the ability of the owner/managers. The amounts of any loan or financing required should be clearly stated together with a financial analysis of the actual and/or the intended proposal; this analysis should show repayment of the financing, cash flow plans and a 'what if' scenario to demonstrate that a contingency plan has been thought through.

The Business Plan should utilise any information that has already been obtained from carrying out the strategy, marketing and resource analyses. It can become a working internal document for a business, summarising the findings from research and being updated as necessary.

There is no rigid structure that can be applied to any report but there are certain key elements that need to be included. These are described below.

COVERING LETTER

If the report is being sent to external parties then a covering letter should accompany it. This does not need to be overly long but should include the bare essentials:

- The intended recipient.
- The author.
- The nature and name of the business.
- The purpose of the document.
- Confirmation of any agreed meeting.
- Contact details.

TITLE PAGE

The title page should attract the attention whilst staying clear and simple. It should give the name and logo of the business together with the name of the author and the date the report was prepared. It is vital to remember that these are the first parts of the report that anybody will see and creating the right first impression should not be underestimated.

CONTENTS PAGE

The contents page needs to list all the sections of the report with the relevant page numbers. It should also include the location of any diagrams or tables and the contents of any appendices.

EXECUTIVE SUMMARY

This should be a brief and concise overview of the entire document and therefore needs to be prepared last. It needs to be helpful to the reader, allowing him or her to make a quick decision, and it should allow you to convey your commitment to and excitement about the business. It should refer to the organisation concerned, the reasons for the proposal, amounts of any financing required and a summary of intended margins and repayment.

CURRENT MARKET SITUATION

This should be a brief explanation of the relevant industry and related sectors. For example if the report is being produced for a business within the livery sector, it is necessary to include a background of the equine industry as a whole together with specific information relating to livery yards. The report should assume that the reader knows nothing and must not include any 'jargon'. It should include an assessment of existing customers if this is relevant, new markets being targeted and information relating to competitors. If market analysis has been carried out then the results should be given. Details will be required about the current market share and anticipated growth. In order for the reader to gain confidence in the information supplied it is useful to reference any statistics to their source, with any details supplied in the appendices.

EXISTING BUSINESS

If the Business Plan is being written for an existing business then a detailed description is an essential part of the business planning process. This should include a brief history explaining the products or services that are currently available, an explanation of the management team with details regarding key staff, and a summary of the current strategy.

PROPOSED DEVELOPMENT

This should be a detailed explanation of the business or proposal, to allow the reader to understand what is required. This can relate to a stand-alone project, or the future of the existing business. If different options were discussed before arriving at the final decision, it can be useful to summarise the decision making process and any assumptions that have been made. This allows the final justification to be presented in a structured format. If a project is part of a larger overall development, then this contribution needs to be made clear. Long-term projections can be referred to if they are part of the business strategy. For example the building of an indoor school will have a short, medium and long term effect on the overall business and should be included under these headings in a report setting out the justification for the project.

PROJECT SCHEDULE

If the plan is being produced for a particular project then it is vital to show key events together with the planned timescale. Even for an existing business, it is useful to put dates and timescales to future activity. This timetable may need to be split into different sections, perhaps pre-launch, launch and post-launch for a new product, setting out the responsibilities and events under each section. Any critical events which are dependent on the completion of other events must be clearly highlighted. Within the risk assessment section of the report, reference can then be made to an alternative course of action should the need arise.

MARKETING PLAN

If a full Marketing Plan has been produced, as discussed in Chapter 9, then this section of the Business Plan can refer to it. The key points should be summarised and take into account the five Ps of Product/Price/Place/Promotion and People, showing details of any pricing plan, how any new or amended product/service will be sold and the advertising strategy that is to take place. It should provide a clear point of reference for the marketing activities of the business.

FINANCE PLAN

This may be one of the largest sections, and should contain details of actual and budgeted income and expenditure, together with cash flow analyses. It should indicate actual and expected margins, together with expected future growth and the break-even point in terms of profitability. It may be useful to show a summary within the main body of the report and a detailed breakdown in the appendices.

CRITICAL RISK ASSESSMENT

This should cover the 'what if' scenarios, indicating potential risks within the business or project and what actions will be taken if they arise. This assessment should cover the factors internal and external to the business.

SENSITIVITY ANALYSIS

This section should show how sensitive the projected margins, income or expenses are to changes in one or more of the variables. For example if sales are higher or lower than expected, if the volume is higher or lower than expected or if costs are higher or lower than expected.

APPENDICES

These should contain any in-depth analysis required and should be cross-referenced within the body of the report. Detailed breakdowns may be required for the following areas:

- Budgets.
- Cash flow forecasts.
- Profit and loss accounts.
- Balance sheets.
- Quotes for project expenditure.
- Curriculum vitae for key staff.
- Key references to external material.

Part 3
Case Studies

Case study 1: The small DIY yard

Mr Smith owns a 250 acre mixed farm in the Cotswolds with a further 100 acres of grassland rented from a nearby estate. He has been encouraged to diversify into equine business by his friend in the next village who has a successful small livery business on his property. He has a stone barn which could be converted into 10 stables and 20 acres of grassland adjacent to the yard suitable for horse paddocks. He has all the skills and machinery necessary for maintaining the grazing land. He also makes hay and haylage and produces his own straw which he plans to sell to livery clients.

He has some experience with horses; he owns a 12-year-old Point to Point mare who he puts to a National Hunt stallion each year and sells the yearlings at the sales. The area has a thriving equestrian community and a network of good off road rides.

His neighbour has also diversified. He runs a pheasant shoot in the valley overlooking the Smith's farmyard.

THE FACILITIES

- Stone barn suitable for conversion to 10 internal stables.
- 20 acres of good grazing adjacent to the farmyard.
- Access to a further 230 acres of mixed farmland with set aside allowing safe off road riding.
- Easy access to additional safe riding.
- Ample hard standing for parking.

ENVIRONMENTAL ANALYSIS

A business of this size is unlikely to carry out a full scale environmental analysis. It is much more realistic to expect the manager to make a more specific assessment of his immediate environment. The SWOT analysis is an excellent tool for this situation; it is a concise and efficient way of examining the good and bad points of both the internal and external environment.

Strengths

- The easy access to safe off road riding is an important factor for recreational riders. Aside from the 250 acres of farmland there is also a good local network of bridleways and, where it is necessary to go on the road, many of the local roads are quiet.

- The sale of hay, haylage and straw on site is convenient for the liveries and provides an extra income stream for the farm. Because the forage is made on site it will be of a consistent quality.

- Mr Smith has all the equipment and knowledge necessary to maintain the paddocks and the fencing to the highest standard.

- The stone barn is ideal for conversion into stables. The large roof space and wide barn doors will allow excellent ventilation and the traditional construction is very attractive.

- The local equestrian services are excellent. There are several experienced farriers in the area, an equine veterinary clinic 15 miles away and two saddlers in the nearest town.

- The farm is situated on the border between the Beaufort and Vale of White Horse hunt countries.

- There are a number of competition venues within an easy drive.

- Smith has a knowledge of horses, having owned a string of brood mares over the last 20 years.

- Because Smith has a public footpath across his land he already has public liability insurance. The certificate is displayed in the farm office.

Weaknesses

- Although Smith has owned horses for many years he has no experience of riding and no understanding of the needs of riders. He is ill prepared to deal with the demanding nature of recreational riders.

- There are no toilet facilities in the farm yard so he may well have clients knocking on his door in times of need.

- There is only one entrance to the farmyard that must be shared by both livery clients and farm traffic. Horses and tractors do not always mix and this could lead to a conflict of interests between farm staff and horse owners.

- The barn will need some work on the roof before the stables can be constructed. This will require a capital outlay and it could be some months before any income is brought in.

- The rest of the farmyard is in need of some attention, particularly the 'farm implement grave yard' behind the potential stables. Piles of rubbish can be a hazard to escaped horses and children.

Opportunities

- There may well be grants available for doing up the stone barn.

- Two other barns are suitable for conversion in the future and there are a further 10 acres that are suitable for grazing horses.

- One of the bigger livery yards in the vicinity is currently up for sale. One of the potential purchasers plans to turn it into a stud if the sale goes through; this means that there will be 30 livery clients looking for a new yard.

Threats

- The threat to hunting is likely to have far reaching consequences for the entire equine industry but, as yet, it is impossible to predict just how much of an impact it will have on each sector of the industry.

- The existing livery yards in the area are already well established.

- As a farm business Smith has not had to worry about the issues of business rates but as a livery yard he will be expected to pay them on the buildings that are utilised for the equine business. Although there is a rate relief scheme currently in place for farm diversification projects it is only a temporary measure and the business will have to pay rates in full after the initial time period has elapsed.

- The neighboring shoot is active throughout the shooting season and although it does not actually venture too close to the border with Smith's farm the bangs are very audible and could startle horses. The pheasants also roam across both properties and have a tendency to erupt from hedgerows at inopportune moments.

ISSUES WARRANTING FURTHER INVESTIGATION

Health and safety issues

Although by law Smith is not obliged to have a health and safety policy document because he has fewer than five employees he would be well advised to have carried out a risk assessment for both horses and clients. This should cover potential danger areas such as machinery, agri-chemicals and fire. He will need to make some provision for fire safety and first aid equipment and get professional advice regarding public liability and insurance.

Traffic

The farm vehicles and the livery clients will have to use the same drive-way so both parties will need to be tolerant of the other. It is important for the tractor drivers to be aware of the effect that tractors and machinery can have on horses and also for the livery clients to understand that many farm operations are weather sensitive and so often need to be accomplished as quickly as possible before the weather turns inclement.

The human factor

Although Smith and his wife are gregarious people they may not fully appreciate the impact that a continuous stream of horse owners will have on their lives. Horse owners can be a very demanding group and are likely to disturb him on a regular basis with queries about broken fences, forage and bedding supplies and other assorted matters. Although these issues may seem trivial and irritating to him he must understand that these people are his clients and are paying him for a service. He must also be prepared to deal with cars parked in daft places, random visitors, farriers, dogs, children, equipment scattered around the yard and a variety of other unforeseen occurrences.

STRATEGY

Smith is ideally positioned to implement a cost leadership strategy for a number of reasons:

- As he already owns the facilities he has no rent to pay.
- He has access to a ready supply of straw, haylage and hay produced at home at cost price.

- He already owns the necessary equipment to maintain the pasture and it has already been written off in the accounts so does not owe the farm anything. Any replacement costs will go through on the farm accounts.

Implementation

For a business to follow a successful cost leadership strategy it has to have some method of generating a financial advantage over its competitors. This can be achieved in any number of ways but usually involves either lower business expenses or better utilisation of resources.

First Smith must find out who his closest competitors are and find out what level of service they are offering. He then needs to find out how much they are charging for their services. This will give him a benchmark price.

Next he needs to work out exactly how much it will cost him to provide the service. Here he must consider:

- The actual capital cost of converting the buildings into stables.

- The proportion of the telephone, power and water bills that is attributable to the stables.

- The proportion of vehicle use that is directly related to the equine enterprise, including the relevant part of the cost of fuel and maintenance. This must also be included in the price of the hay and straw that are sold on to liveries.

- There will be occasions when farm staff will be drafted into use on the yard. This will need to be taken into account when setting the prices.

- There is likely to be an increase in insurance.

- The business rates will need to be taken into account even though they may not be incurred for several years.

- Finally he must consider the value of both his and his wife's time.

Having worked out what price range he needs to hold in order to be competitive with the best in the market and then made certain that he can offer and maintain that low price while still making a profit, it is important that he does not just sit back and leave the yard to its own devices.

In order to maintain a good profit margin he needs to continue to monitor all his relevant expenses. This means that he will need to keep accurate records of costs and hours invested in the enterprise. He will also need to pay close attention to the activities of his rivals in order to ensure that he stays competitive.

Potential pitfalls

As with any strategy there are some pitfalls that need to be avoided:

- If the yard is supplying or selling forage and bedding materials as part of the service there may be some loss of income to the farm from these sales. The farm needs to acknowledge that it could be necessary to get a less than optimum income from these sales in order to maximise the benefits from the strategy.

- It is important to try to at least acknowledge that there are almost always other things that could be done with the facilities and that these alternatives could yield a higher income. This is called the opportunity cost.

- It is vitally important if this strategy is to succeed to have systems in place to accurately track costs and cash flow. This is the only way to make sure that the strategy is being adhered to and is succeeding in its aims.

MARKETING

As has been mentioned several times there is very little in the way of formal marketing strategy that is currently practised in the equine livery industry. However, whatever business strategy a yard pursues it is, to a certain extent, aiming its service at a specific segment of the market. It is therefore important to correctly identify who is being targeted and how to communicate with them.

For a yard pursuing a cost leadership strategy the target segment is likely to be hackers and pleasure riders from the surrounding area. For Smith there is no point trying to target competition riders because he has none of the facilities required to train a competition horse. His yard is, however, ideally suited to the requirements of the leisure rider, with access to safe off road hacking, good quality and competitively priced forage and bedding, and low charges.

Research has suggested that the majority of livery yards were recommended to their clients rather than attracting their attention by adverts. This serves to reinforce the point that the main form of communication within the industry is by word of mouth and the best advert for a yard is satisfied customers.

Any additional advertising should be aimed specifically at the target market: local recreational riders. It is therefore a waste of money to run adverts in a national magazine such as *Horse and Hound* but could be beneficial to advertise in local tack shops and riding club magazines.

Case study 2: The small competition yard

Mike rents 'The Stables' from neighbouring farmer Mr Thomas. The yard is a self-contained unit originally developed for Mr Thomas's daughter who has now got married and moved away. The yard is in Warwickshire, an attractive part of the English countryside with an established equine infrastructure. He has a one-year tenancy agreement, which is renewed annually every October. He has currently been there for three years.

Mike is a well respected member of the local equestrian community with a wide circle of friends and good people skills. He is also a capable event rider who brings on young horses to sell. He currently has three young thoroughbreds, bought from the Ascot sales, in various stages of competition readiness although one is off work with an abscess in the foot. He part owns one advanced horse and competes an intermediate for another owner. Both these horses are aiming for three-day events this year. The intermediate horse is a stallion that returns to his owner's stud from March through to the end of May.

Mike has four part liveries, one of which is owned by Karen, a local student, who helps Mike during her spare time in return for free livery. He also takes on short term break and school liveries. Although he is not on the BHS register of instructors he teaches seven other riders on a regular basis, including Karen.

THE FACILITIES

- Converted barn containing 10 internal stables.
- Adequate storage for tack and feed but limited space for forage and bedding.
- Five acres of grazing adjacent to the yard.
- Access to mixed farmland with set aside allowing safe off road riding.
- Standard 40 × 20 outdoor school.

- Some space for parking lorries and clients' cars but the access is hampered by a narrow gateway.
- One bedroom flat above the tack and feed room.
- Small set of show jumps.

ENVIRONMENTAL ANALYSIS

Like Mr Smith, it is unlikely that Mike will have the time or the inclination to carry out a wide-ranging and comprehensive analysis of all three of the environmental sectors that affect his business. Although there are several aspects of the external environment, such as tenancy and health and safety legislation, and many competitive environment issues that will have a direct impact on his business, a well thought out SWOT analysis will still be an excellent starting place. It may be necessary to then take a closer look at some of the key issues raised.

Strengths

- The depth of knowledge and experience that Mike has built up over the years is the business's key asset. As a professional rider he has gained a reputation as a reliable and consistent rider who produces well mannered and schooled young horses, and his gregarious nature and open manner have allowed him to generate a firm client base and excellent list of contacts.

- The safe off road riding, in the arena or around the adjacent farm land, is ideal for preparing young horses and carrying out competition fitness work.

- The local equine infrastructure allows easy access to experienced vets and farriers as well as a selection of tack shops and feed merchants.

- The yard itself is well laid out and maintained, which allows Mike to work in an efficient manner.

- Both the owners of Mike's competition horses are supportive and knowledgeable. The horses themselves are both showing promise and the whole team is optimistic about the up and coming three-day events.

- Karen is happy to act as Mike's unofficial groom and working pupil and is more than capable of handling all the horses in the yard. She has a good relationship with Mike's owners and liveries.

- Mike has a four-horse HGV lorry with living. It is in a reasonable state of repair.

- Mike's experience means that he can offer a high level of service to his clients while still being flexible enough to tailor the service to their needs.

Weaknesses

- The yard is restricted to only 5 acres of grazing. There is no question of extending the amount of adjacent grazing available because the surrounding land is all arable and is subject to a contract farming agreement with another farmer. If Mike needs more grass keep he will have to look further afield for it.

- Although Mike is an excellent horseman he has very few business skills. His financial record keeping leaves a lot to be desired and although he is excellent at planning his horses' competition schedule he has no concept of business planning.

- The lorry is an HGV and Mike is the only person who can drive it.

- The landlord tends to be very slow when it comes to carrying out essential repairs and maintenance work.

- Mike buys the young horses on a tight budget but because he is buying and selling on such a small scale he cannot really afford to make a loss on any of them. The critical success factors for this part of the business are therefore very tight. The horse that is currently off work with an abscess could well end up having a serious effect on this section of Mike's budget.

- Most of Mike's teaching is 'cash in hand' which usually does not make it as far as the books. This could have severe repercussions should the tax man start to take an interest in Mike's affairs.

Opportunities

- As an active competition rider Mike is in an ideal position to show off and sell his young horses and also to attract new clients. He is also able to stay abreast of developments on the eventing circuit.

- Although there are several other competition riders based in the area, Mike has by far the best reputation with young or difficult horses. There is therefore an opportunity to develop this side of the business.

- Mike's reputation as an event rider has contributed to his standing as an instructor. There is some demand for him to start teaching clinics at other locations. Although this will mean that he has to spend some time away from his own yard the financial benefits would more than compensate for the occasional need to pay for extra help. It would also widen his client base and possibly bring in more regular teaching clients.

Threats

- The landowner, although he has indicated to Mike that he is happy with the current arrangement, will only commit to a yearly tenancy agreement. Should he wish to end the tenancy Mike will find it very hard to find comparable properties in the area. There is also the danger that he might want to sharply increase the rent.

- The implications of a ban on hunting are more severe for Mike because his yard is situated in the heart of the Warwickshire hunt country and therefore many of his suppliers rely on the hunt for business. There is a real possibility that, should they lose this business, they will have to make changes to their own prices and business structure. Two of Mike's part liveries are also hunt followers and, although they are unlikely to sell their horses if hunting is banned, they are almost certain to move their horses to a cheaper yard.

- With the current need for farmers to diversify there is a threat of other yards opening up in the vicinity with better facilities. Although Mike is not competing for DIY clients he would be in danger from another rider setting up a similar operation to his own.

- Karen will not be a student forever and is not interested in working with horses full time. When she goes she will leave a big gap in Mike's team. His chances of finding another 'Karen' are very slim. He may have to consider employing someone part time.

- As a 'one man band' Mike's business is reliant on his ability to work, and dealing with young and problem horses can be dangerous. He therefore needs to consider his own situation with regard to accident insurance.

ISSUES WARRANTING FURTHER INVESTIGATION

Health and safety issues

As Mike has no employees he has no legal obligation with regard to health and safety legislation but because he has clients and their horses under his care on the premises he will need to get professional advice about public liability and insurance. There is a further complication in that although Karen is not an employee he must still take responsibility for her welfare when she is helping him on the yard. There is a also the issue of his liability as an instructor because he has no official qualifications and is not an accredited trainer, although he is currently looking into this issue.

Agreements with owners

Mike has no formal agreement with either of his owners. Although he has a good relationship with both of them there is no guarantee that this will continue. Because he owns a share in the advanced horse he thinks that he has a measure of control but in reality he does not own a controlling share so he legally has little say in the horse's future. Were he to lose his two good horses he would be in a difficult position because he relies on his reputation as a competitive rider to get clients. He has also invested a large amount of his time in the horses' development for which he would get no compensation should the horses be taken from him. Although asking for a written agreement at this stage in the relationship could cause a lot of bad feeling he should be aware of the possible cost of having no agreement and consider drafting one for any rides he gains in the future.

Mike's business skills

Mike has no business skills at all. He maintains a healthy client base because he is a talented horseman, an excellent teacher and a genuinely nice person. Because of his current abundance of clients he is making a sensible profit but his lack of administrative ability could cause severe problems if his business was to hit a lean patch.

While he needs to secure the services of a good accountant and also find a reliable source of business advice there are a number of administrative procedures that he should be implementing:

- Keep all receipts for money spent on the business, both cheques and cash.
- Keep all cheque books, paying in books and bank statements.
- Issue invoices for all work done and keep a copy of all invoices issued.
- Monitor payments from customers to ensure no bad debts are allowed to build up.
- Make sure that he is aware of the state of his bank balance at all times.

Mike's lack of business planning also causes time management issues. Because of the seasonal nature of his work he is rushed off his feet for part of the year while at other times he is left kicking his heels. By planning his activities more efficiently he should be able to spread his workload so as to make better use of resources. Encouraging owners to send him their problem horses during the winter, when he has less youngsters to break, will allow him to spend more time with them. This will benefit both Mike and the horses in question.

STRATEGY

Mike is in a position to implement one of two strategies: focus or differentiation. His understanding of the event circuit and his prowess as a rider could have led him to focus his attention on event riders; however, that is not the direction that his business has taken.

Whether through design or accident his business has developed around his skill at producing well mannered young horses and his ability to cater to the needs of individual clients; he has, in this way, differentiated his service from that of his competitors:

- His people skills allow him to communicate effectively with livery and teaching clients. This means that he is able to tailor his services to their exact needs.

- He has exceptional skill with young horses from all disciplines and is happy to work with any youngster, irrespective of their quirks or their owners' goals.

- His reputation with difficult horses means that he draws clients from a wider geographical and discipline area.

- Although his preferred discipline is eventing he has built up a teaching client base from other disciplines as well.

Implementation

For a business to follow a successful differentiation strategy it has to have some method of maintaining an obvious difference between itself and its competitors. In this case the key feature is Mike himself. He has succeeded in gaining a reputation and has built a business around it.

In order to maintain his strong client base it would seem that Mike just needs to keep doing what he is doing but, as with most things in life, it is not that simple. There are several areas that Mike needs to pay attention to if his business is to stay healthy:

- Because he is providing a tailored service to his clients he needs to keep paying close attention to what it is that his clients actually want.

- He must remember that he has three key areas of business: livery, teaching and preparing horses. Each sector has different requirements even though they were attracted to him for similar reasons.

- Because he is providing a specialist service his clients are paying a premium. This means that he is dependent on them maintaining a suitable disposable income. He needs to keep a close eye on his external environment so that he is in a position to react to potential problems before they become real problems.

- Mike needs to pay close attention to what his competitors are doing. Equine clients are notoriously fickle and because Mike's strategy is based around his reputation and ability he needs to be aware of anyone who is attempting to poach his clients and build their own reputation.

Potential pitfalls

There is no such thing as a foolproof strategy and Mike needs to be aware of the problems he may face in order to try to stay ahead of his competitors:

- It is important to remember that a differentiation strategy does not mean that other aspects of the service provided can be overlooked in favour of the key selling point. The focal point of the business is not the only aspect of the business and is only viable if the entire service being supplied stands up to scrutiny. One outstanding feature cannot carry a yard that has nothing else to offer.

- It cannot be overestimated how important it is to keep up to date with what your competitors are doing. It is impossible to retain any sort of competitive advantage if you do not actually know what you are competing against.

MARKETING

The marketing strategy that a business adopts should reflect the business strategy that is in place. It would therefore be counterproductive for Mike to try to promote a business based around a range of talents that appeals to a range of equine clients by attempting to target a small group of them.

It makes much more sense to concentrate on the 'identity' or brand of the product or service being offered. Any yard that is pursuing a differentiation strategy can gain a benefit from developing a brand identity. This marketing strategy is particularly apt in Mike's case because he is, in real terms, the yard and the brand.

By making sure that in all his business and competitive activities his image and actions are consistent, Mike can generate a brand identity and then use the reputation it gains as an advertisement for its service. This can be helped by the use of a consistent colour scheme and logo on rugs, vehicles, riding gear, stationery and invoices, and the use of his name on competition entries.

It is important for Mike to make the most of the advertising opportunity presented by his competing. His appearance in results sections of magazines and competition reports is an ongoing and free source of publicity and is more effective than classified ads.

Case study 3: The commercial livery yard

Amanda and James bought Stable House in Buckinghamshire three years ago when they relocated from New York. James is on the board of a London based corporation and Amanda is in advertising. Amanda gave up riding at university but bought the property with the intention of taking up dressage. Since moving in she has bought three horses, two of which are working at medium level and one is a semi-retired Grand Prix horse bought as a schoolmaster. Although they both commute into London daily Amanda only rides at the weekend.

The yard was built five years ago by the previous owner and although it is very attractive it is not designed to be particularly easy to work in. There are vast expanses of gravel to rake, grass to mow and the muck-heap is a long way from the stables.

The yard is run by Nikki who is a BHSII with an HND from a local agricultural college. She has worked for Amanda for two years and has a young dressage horse of her own which she keeps at the yard. Amanda allows her to do some teaching to supplement her income.

Nikki is helped by five other grooms, three full time and two part time on day release from a local college. Because of the nature of the job – the clients can be overly demanding and the work is routine – the staff turnover is relatively high. Aside from Nikki, the longest serving groom has been there for one year and is now thinking of moving on.

Between the rest of the clients there is a 50/50 split of competitive riders and happy hackers and the two groups do not always see eye to eye. This situation tests Nikki's diplomacy skills to the limit and Amanda does not help by coming in strongly on the side of her fellow dressage riders.

James puts up with horses but tries to have as little to do with them as possible. He is, however, a motor cycle fanatic and has four, ranging from an old Triumph to a new Harley. The bikes live in two of the three garages attached to the house. James has a habit of retreating to the garage and tinkering when he has one of his frequent, vocal disagreements with Amanda. The couple also have two boisterous Labradors, which have the run of the place and tend to fight with any other male dogs that appear on the premises.

THE RESOURCES

- Purpose built American barn containing 30 stables.

- 25 acres of grazing adjacent to the stable yard. James has an ongoing arrangement with a local contractor to carry out any maintenance so the paddocks are in an excellent state of repair.

- Easy access to bridleways.

- A 60 × 20 outdoor arena with floodlights. There is an ATV, harrow and grader to level the surface.

- The horse walker is covered and has a rubber floor.

- The wash box has hot and cold water and a heat lamp.

- The tack room is alarmed and there are security gates at the end of the drive. There are also motion sensor lights all around the yard.

- There is ample hard standing for parking clients' cars, lorries and trailers.

- Nikki is a very professional yard manager who has good organisational skills and exceptional talents as a diplomat. She is assisted by three full time and two part time grooms of various levels of experience.

- A spacious and fully furnished staff cottage which Nikki shares with the other three full time staff.

- A very smart four-horse lorry which James is overly precious about. Nikki is the member of staff who has a licence for it and although Amanda will give clients a lift to competitions she is attending, she will not lend it out.

ENVIRONMENTAL ANALYSIS

Because the external environment can have such a huge impact on the business it would be sensible to expand the environmental analysis. As James has a strong business background it is likely that he has a good grasp of the business environment. However his ideas of profit margins do not sit easily with horses. It is not unrealistic to expect him to do a complete environmental analysis.

External environment

Political factors

- The hunting legislation is likely to have a much greater impact on Amanda's yard than she imagines. Because she does not hunt and has no purely hunting clients she assumes that it is of no consequence to her. She has failed to take into account how it will affect the rest of her industry.

- At Nikki's suggestion Amanda has looked at the BHS livery yard registration scheme but has not yet got around to doing anything about it. In the event of a compulsory livery yard registration scheme being brought in she is confident that her yard will meet all the criteria.

Economic factors

- Because Amanda and James are both high earners with adequate investments the yard does not currently have to provide them with an income. However, should their financial position change significantly this situation will have to change. James insists that the horses at least pay for themselves and is well aware of how much money is spent on them; he is equally aware of the earning potential of the yard.

- Because the yard offers a certain level of service coupled with excellent facilities it is able to charge a premium rate. For this reason the majority of the clients are themselves high earners. They are as susceptible to changes in the economic climate as James and Amanda. This situation means that the whole balance of the yard is tightly allied to the financial markets and state of the economy.

Social factors

- Nikki is currently settled at Stable House. She enjoys the level of responsibility and appreciates the fact that Amanda is supportive of her competitive aspirations.

- Amanda has continuing issues with staff turnover amongst the more junior members of staff. The nature of the job, the long hours and the occasionally excessive demands of some of the clients can be demoralising. The frequent and often petty sniping between the hackers and the competitive riders causes a strained atmosphere which upsets the younger members of staff and often puts Nikki in a difficult position.

- Clients appreciate continuity of staff and it would be well worth Amanda making the effort to reduce the level of turnover. It is unrealistic to expect her to sort out her warring liveries, although it would help a lot if she did not let herself get so involved in the dispute. She could also ask them to show more respect to the staff and look at offering the junior staff more perks. These could include training towards exams, lessons, increased pay and more time off.

Technical factors

- The horse walker allows all the liveries to get some walking exercise during the day while the staff are doing other jobs. This cuts down drastically on the time that they spend doing other forms of exercise. This in turn cuts down on the number of staff needed to provide care for them.

Legal factors

- Because Amanda has more than five employees she is required by law to have a health and safety policy document because the overall responsibly for the health and safety of the staff lies with Amanda. She needs to make sure that everyone on the yard, including clients and visiting service providers, is aware of the document. She must display a summary of the document, setting out individual responsibilities, in a public place, such as the tack room or coffee room. She must have a human first aid box and a trained first aider and she must be aware of all the relevant regulations. She must also have performed risk assessments for, amongst other things, fire hazards, any machinery on site, use of chemicals and drugs, and the safe handling of horses, and have emergency procedures in place.

- James insists that all clients sign a livery contract. This states where the yard's responsibility begins and ends and sets out the billing procedure and price structure. It also informs the clients of the steps that the yard will take in the event of any problems arising. Amanda also insists that all the horses are insured for vets' fees and reserves the right to call the vet if necessary.

- Nikki's teaching is all cash in hand and it is her responsibility to see that this income is declared to the tax man.

Competitive environment

Suppliers

Amanda and her liveries spend a lot of money on their horses. James has used his business sense to use this fact to their advantage and has negotiated favourable rates with the local feed merchant and the farmer who supplies hay and haylage. He has also managed to arrange an account with an equine products wholesaler for the supply of wormers, shampoos, poultices and other products in the wholesaler's range. The local tack shop and veterinary practice also allow them to run a yard account and give them a business discount.

Customers

Amanda's clients pay a premium for the level of service and facility that they receive. Because of the level of charges they are, in turn, very vocal when they perceive that they are not getting what they have paid for. They also have a lot of contact with livery clients from other establishments, both socially and at competitions, and are often quick to mention any improvements that their acquaintances have benefited from. This drives Amanda and Nikki to stay ahead of their game in order to maintain the reputation of the yard.

New entrants to the industry

The amount of capital necessary to build a yard like Stable House when compared to the expected return on the investment is a significant barrier to entry. However, Amanda does have to be aware of the dangers presented by existing yards upping the level of facility and service that they offer.

Competitors

As has already been mentioned Amanda and Nikki are frequently reminded by their clients of the level of service, facilities and price offered by their competitors. If they are to keep their clients happy and sustain their position in the market they have to be careful to maintain their high standards.

STRATEGY

Amanda and James chose Stable House because it was, in Amanda's eyes, ideally suited to her aspirations as a dressage rider. Since moving in she has focused all her equestrian activities, including the development of the livery business, on this aim. In this way she has implemented a focus strategy.

Although she has no formal mission statement or goals Amanda has a very clear idea of the requirements of her target audience because they are so closely allied to her own and is able to charge a premium rate in recognition of the specifically tailored service. The fact that nearly half her clients are not actually competitive dressage riders is a source of minor annoyance to her.

Implementation

Amanda's enthusiasm and drive has been targeted towards dressage since she first started looking for a yard. Her own personal focus has led her to consciously position her establishment in the competition livery sector of the market, and specifically the dressage sector of the competition livery bracket.

She has fulfilled the criteria for implementing a successful focus strategy in almost every way:

- The facilities that she offers are geared towards the training of dressage horses.

- The yard is situated in an affluent area where the prospective clients can afford to pay a premium for a service geared towards their needs.

- Dressage is a popular sport in the area and so there is an established client base.

- Both Nikki and Amanda are enthusiastic about dressage and understand the specific problems that are involved in the sport. They can converse with the clients in the correct lingo and are always keen to congratulate and commiserate with them.

- Because both Amanda and Nikki compete on the dressage circuit they are able to stay up to date with the current affairs of the sport. They are also able to find out what is happening in rival yards. This allows them to make certain that their yard is still fulfilling the requirements of the sport and participants and is maintaining its position in the market.

Potential pitfalls

Amanda has addressed, whether by accident or design, almost all the areas that need to be considered when implementing a focus strategy. There is, however, one significant strategic issue that she seems determined to ignore: her non-dressage clients.

- Although only 50% of her clients come from her target audience Amanda still arranges the yard around their specific needs. This means that she is effectively alienating the remaining 50% of her customers. Should one of her competitors start to offer a comparable but less 'dressage orientated' service she runs the risk of losing this group of clients.

- Because she is aiming at a very specific, and therefore narrow, section of the market she is leaving herself very little room to manoeuvre should she hit a problem. She would be very vulnerable to any drastic shifts in the behaviour of that market. It is therefore even more vital for her to keep up to date with developments in the sport.

MARKETING

A yard which has implemented a focus strategy has already opted to appeal to a particular segment of the market. It should, by definition, have a complete understanding of its target market. Both Amanda and Nikki have a very clear idea of the type of person that they are targeting and should therefore have a good appreciation of how best to communicate with them.

The nature of Amanda's business means that she has designed her product to suit the needs of her chosen segment of the population: dressage riders with a significant amount of disposable income who live in a 20 mile radius of her establishment. She has several ways of promoting her business to her target market:

- She can place adverts in dressage magazines. This will fulfil one of her segmentation criteria, dressage riders, but will reach riders from all over the country as opposed to those in her immediate area. The cost of the advert may not be warranted when the potential gains are considered.

- She can place adverts in her local tack shop but again this will reach riders from a wider segment of the market than required. This is not always a bad thing but as Amanda is so keen to attract dressage clients it may not help in this case.

As has been said before, there are more ways to market a product that just placing adverts. Amanda needs to find a way of communicating specifically with her target clients:

- She can rely on word of mouth recommendations from her current clients.

- She can actively promote her yard at the competitions she attends. One of the best ways of doing this is to use the lorry to promote the brand identity of the yard by having the name and contact details prominently displayed. This is, however, out of the question in this case because neither James nor Amanda want to turn the lorry into a 'mobile bill board'. Amanda already has fully colour-coordinated rugs and equipment but does not want to link this to the yard. She would rather keep her competition activities separate from the rest of the yard.

- Possibly the most effective way of attracting local dressage riders would be to invite her dressage trainer to hold regular clinics at the yard.

Case study 4: The equestrian centre

The Big Manor House with its 300 acres and established equestrian centre was bought 6 months ago by The Big Corporation Plc (TBC). The original intention was to keep the house and some of the grounds as a conference and training centre and then sell The Equestrian Centre (TEC) but at the time of the purchase a change on the board led to some different ideas and the new plan is to keep TEC and run it as a competition venue and livery yard.

TEC is now run as a wholly owned subsidiary of TBC. The management structure consists of a business manager responsible for the finance, marketing and administration who is the interface between the yard and the corporation, together with the yard manager responsible for day-to-day activities of the yard. Because TEC is a limited company it has a board of directors which consists of the business manager, the yard manager and a chairman who is also on the board of TBC.

The centre is located in Cheshire, an expanding equine area with excellent access to the motorway network.

Aside from the livery business TEC is a thriving competition venue and holds affiliated dressage and showjumping competitions throughout the year. It also holds affiliated horse trials in the spring and regularly hosts riding club events and hunter trials. The facilities are also utilised for clinics and demonstrations and are hired out by private individuals for schooling.

THE RESOURCES

- Two separate self contained yards containing 30 stables each. Each yard is purpose built and is laid out to facilitate effective yard management. One yard is entirely DIY livery and the other is a mix of part, full and competition.

- 60 acres of grazing with a tractor and assorted implements for grass-land management. An outside contractor comes in to carry out any spraying in the spring and to trim the hedges in the autumn.

- There are two barns which are used for storage of hard food, forage and bedding. They are both clad on three sides but only one has a concrete floor.

- 60 × 25 outdoor school with floodlights which has recently been resurfaced.

- 60 × 40 indoor arena with gallery, lights and watering system and a covered collecting area adjacent.

- Two horse walkers, one in each yard. Both have rubber floors but neither has a roof.

- Two wash down areas in each yard.

- Alarmed tack storage and CCTV in lorry park.

- Separate car parking for livery and competition clients.

- The business manager and the yard manager are assisted by four full time staff and two part time staff.

- Two staff cottages which are well maintained and fully furnished.

- BE novice and pre novice cross-country course.

- Full set of BSJA show jumps.

ENVIRONMENTAL ANALYSIS

TBC has an ongoing programme of environmental impact assessment for its core business activities and its subsidiaries. It constantly monitors any external factors that may affect it so as to be able to pre-empt any decrease in its profit margins. It does not actually carry out a full PEST analysis but employs specialist analysts. TEC is not one of its most profitable subsidiaries but is nevertheless considered to be an asset. During the time of the purchase the external factors most likely to impact the profitability of the yard were examined. There were a number of potential impacts that were considered to be of particular importance.

External environment

Political factors

- The potential change to the law regarding foxhunting will undoubtedly have a major impact on the equine industry as a whole. It has been recommended that any strategy put in place for TEC does not count on any hunting related income and is flexible enough to adapt to the changes that this legislation may cause. This issue warrants careful monitoring.

- Because TEC is a subsidiary it will not be directly affected by political changes in the world arena. However any factors that affect its parent company will have some impact on it and this needs to be acknowledged. There are a large number of political issues that TBC is currently monitoring closely and these include the expansion of the European Union and its effect on the Euro, and the UK general election in 2005.

Economic factors

- The livery clients come from a wide range of backgrounds and professions. This means that they will all be affected by a change in the economic climate in different ways and at different times. TBC has a large department that monitors economic change and its effects on both its core business and subsidiary companies.

- The clients and staff of TEC should also be aware that any change in the economic climate may well have an effect on the policy of TBC. Although TBC currently plans to keep TEC there is no guarantee that this will continue indefinitely. TEC is a valuable resource which could be sold off as a going concern should TBC need to generate some capital or cash flow.

- All horses at TEC are bedded on shavings which are purchased in bulk. They occasionally have difficulties with their supplier and the yard manager was shocked to find that the supply of wood shavings was closely allied to the house building market and that this was the reason for the fluctuations in supply.

Social factors

- The team is generally close knit and well motivated. The pay is good by equine standards, the yard is pleasant to work in and the regular competitions mean that there is enough variation to provide interest.

The staff accommodation is clean and well laid out but because the yard manager has to share with the junior staff there is occasional friction. The staff turnover is unusually low.

- TEC has a comprehensive staff training programme which offers preparation for BHS exams. It also actively encourages staff to further their careers by allowing them six training days per year for which they receive full pay. This allows them time to pursue qualifications that particularly interest them such as dressage judging and showjump course building.

Technological factors

- TEC makes full use of the Internet in all its competition planning. It accepts entries over the Net, publishes a full competition schedule and has a regularly updated website. This has drastically reduced the work load in the office.

- The security devices in use around the yard are developed by another of TBC's subsidiaries and are state of the art. This has led to a favourable reduction in contents insurance for TEC.

Legal factors

- TBC has a health and safety policy in place which includes the activities of TEC and is implemented by the appointed health and safety officer. He is in charge of organising induction training for all new members of staff. The yard manager carries out this training for the stable staff and makes sure that they are aware of the risks involved in the use of all machinery, handling of drugs and chemicals, horse management and any other relevant operations.

- The yard has four separate first aid kits and four of the staff members have attended a first aid at work course. This is in excess of the legal requirements but TBC considers that horses are dangerous and wishes to take appropriate precautions.

- The local fire brigade has visited and carried out a fire risk assessment. It has recommended a fire safety action plan which has been implemented. The fire brigade has also carried out a fire fighting demonstration which all staff attended. It holds regular fire drills and the extinguishers are serviced as necessary. All electrical equipment is checked annually by an approved contractor.

- All livery clients are expected to sign a standard contract.

- TBC has public liability cover and employer's liability cover. The certificates are displayed in the stable office.

- Because of the size of TBC the accounts for TEC are handled in-house by the finance department.

- All competitions are held under the rules and regulations of the relevant sports governing bodies.

- TEC has recently had to invest a significant sum of money to make sure that its premises meet the required standards of disabled access. This has involved creating ramps, building a new toilet facility and moving the office to a ground floor location.

Competitive environment

Suppliers

The volume of business generated by TEC means that it is in a strong position to bargain with its equestrian suppliers. The business manager has a proven track record in business to business negotiations and has managed to achieve favourable deals with most of his main suppliers:

- Because of the volume of horse feed that TEC uses it is able to deal directly with an equine feed manufacturer which delivers once a month. It then sells feed to its DIY clients at a small mark up.

- Like Stable House, TEC has an agreement in place with an equine wholesaler. Most of the products are then sold on to the clients at a small profit. However, some, such as shampoos, are included in the cost of the part, full and competition livery.

- Although TEC is a large equine business it can bring no pressure to bear on multi-national companies such as its fuel supplier. It does, however, benefit from some of the deals that TBC has negotiated. For example it is able to purchase its computer equipment at a discount through TBC.

Competitors

Because TEC is both a competition venue and a livery yard it has to pay attention to two different types of competitor:

- As a competition venue it faces a challenge from other competition venues across a wide geographical location. When riders have a choice of venue there is a variety of factors that will affect their decision and these factors will alter based on what type of competition they are attending. They will consider not only the standard of the facilities but also the standard of the judging, the degree of difficulty of the course, the likely standard of the other competitors, the efficiency of the organisation and the suitability of the classes.

- As a livery yard TEC is in the enviable position of having a massive advantage over its competitors because of the level of its facilities. Because of this factor and the reputation of its yard manager it has a waiting list for both yards. Its two nearest rivals both have arenas but one is prone to flooding and neither are floodlit due to restrictions imposed by the planning authority.

Customers

- Because TEC currently has a waiting list for both its yards its livery clients can exert very little pressure. However, should the yard try to capitalise on this situation by increasing its prices by more than the market will bear then the clients will vote with their feet.

- The competition clients have, however, a number of other alternatives and this provides an incentive for TEC to maintain the high standards of its competition facilities.

New entrants to the industry

The size and scope of this facility means that there are a number of barriers that anyone wishing to compete with them will need to overcome:

- The size of the property is a limiting factor; there are very few plots of land of this type likely to come up for sale in the near future.
- The amount of capital necessary to build a yard like TEC is far beyond the resources of most equine businesses.
- Should someone acquire the necessary land and finances they will still have to overcome the local planning regulations.

STRATEGY

Before TBC made its decision to keep TEC it carried out a full strategic review of the business. This process highlighted the lack of management planning or strategic direction that was present under the previous management regime. The report recommended that the business needed to make drastic changes to its method of operation if it was to develop into the profitable enterprise that it should be.

The first step was to completely restructure the management of the business. Under the previous owners the head girl had been expected to take much of the responsibility for the office management. These additional responsibilities were outside her area of expertise and took up too much of her time. As a result she was overstretched and stressed. The rest of the office work was carried out by the bookkeeper, who came in once a week, a part time secretary and the owner. There was no management structure and jobs were done as and when they became urgent.

TBC has appointed a business manager to take full responsibility for all aspects of running TEC as a business. His remit is to address all areas of business management including the introduction of a strategic plan, to increase the marketing of the establishment and to increase efficiency and profitability. He is assisted by a part time secretary.

TEC has continued to employ the head girl but her area of responsibility has been redefined. She is now able to concentrate on the management of the two stable yards and the facilities. She works closely with the business manager and he defers to her on all equine matters.

TEC has a tag line that appears at the bottom of all its paperwork and on any advertisements it places:

THE EQUESTRIAN CENTRE:
CATERING FOR ALL THE NEEDS OF THE COMPETITIVE HORSE AND RIDER

It has a series of short term objectives. These are intended to be achieved during this calendar year:

- To maintain maximum occupancy of both livery yards.
- To run one affiliated showjumping and dressage competition each month.
- To run one affiliated horse trials.
- To run one unaffiliated showjumping and dressage competition each month.
- To decrease the number of competitions run by outside organisations without decreasing the number of events held here.
- To run two riding clinics per month with accredited trainers.
- To run one demonstration per month.

The majority of these objectives have been achieved.

It also has a series of long term objectives. These are intended to be achieved in the next five years:

- To upgrade the event course to enable BE intermediate events to be held and to increase the number of affiliated events held to two: one in the spring and one in the autumn.

- To hold both dressage and showjumping second round competitions.

- To increase the number of affiliated shows in both disciplines to two per month and increase the level of classes held.

- To increase both the number and profile of the clinics held.

- To extend the scope of the clinics to include other practitioners such as equine dentists, physiotherapists, equine nutrition advisers and problem behaviour specialists.

- To maintain the occupancy of the yard but increase the percentage of clients that are using the higher level of service.

The strategic review document noted that because of the resources that TEC had available it was already attracting clients from a particular part of the equine market but recommended that the business would be best advised to utilise its strengths to differentiate itself from its competitors rather than to increase its level of specialisation.

The optimum strategic direction was, therefore, determined to be one of differentiation.

Implementation

The business manager has drawn up a detailed action plan for achieving the strategic objectives. In it he sets out what needs to be accomplished, who is to be responsible for each target and the time frame involved. All the staff have had the opportunity to read the document and have been invited to express their opinions.

The short-term objectives are achievable and the relative actions have already been taken to make sure that the targets are met. It is the longer-term objectives that occupy the majority of the report.

The business manager sees the yard's competitive activities as the key to maintaining a competitive differentiation and this is reflected in the objectives that have been set. He is of the opinion that by increasing the status of the competition venue he will automatically attract more competition livery clients.

Because many of the long term objectives are dependent on the levels of affiliated competition that he can run, he has already invested a significant amount of time in networking with people from the relevant organisations but until the yard has completed its first full year of operation under the new management they are unwilling to make any commitments.

He has also begun negotiations with an equine nutritionist and a behavioural specialist with the intention of asking them to hold regular clinics. He has, as yet, had no success finding a respected trainer to teach on a regular basis.

Potential pitfalls

The key to this strategy is the increased level of affiliated competition. The increase in livery income, instruction clinics and demonstrations all rely on the increased profile of the centre through its competition activities. There is currently no back up plan should this not be achieved.

The business manager is not overly concerned because all the indications he has received from clients and visiting judges have been positive. He is prepared to see out the season before he makes any drastic reassessments.

MARKETING

The business manager has devised a full marketing strategy for the business. The key aim is to strengthen the brand identity and then use it to promote all the business activities:

- The manager has commissioned a local design company to design a logo which now appears on all the business stationery, in all adverts, on the website, on the rosettes that are handed out at all the competitions and on the staff clothing.

- All clinics and demonstrations are advertised in both the local papers and the national equine press. The adverts all follow the same format and include both the logo and the company tag line (see p. 150) as well as full contact details.

- Anyone who attends a competition or demonstration is added to the business mailing list and receives a quarterly events schedule and newsletter.

- The website is regularly updated with upcoming events and results of recent competitions.

- The local press and national horse magazines are always supplied with a report of each event and the full results sheet.

Every effort is made to see that in all its dealings with the public TEC presents an image of calm efficiency.

References and further reading

References

Bacon, R. (Ed.) (2002) *Equine Business Guide*. Warwickshire College, UK.

BETA (1999a) *National Equestrian Survey: Overview Report*. British Equestrian Trade Association.

BETA (1999b) *National Equestrian Survey: Structural Report*. British Equestrian Trade Association.

BETA (2002) The British Equestrian Trade Association Submission to the Committee of Enquiry into Hunting With Dogs.
www.huntinginquiry.gov.uk/mainsections/huntingframe.htm
(accessed 21/10/02).

Clausewitcz, Von, C. (1968) *On War*. Penguin Books.

Cornwell, B. (1998) *Sharpe's Tiger*. Harper Collins.

Dibb, S., Simkin, L., Pride, W.M. and Ferrell, O.C. (2001) *Marketing Concepts and Strategies*, 4th edn. Houghton Mifflin.

Grant, R.M. (2002) *Contemporary Strategy Analysis*, 4th edn. Blackwell Publishing.

Handy, C. (1995) *Gods of Management*. Arrow Books.

Health and Safety Executive (2002) *Control of Substances Harmful to Health*.
www.hse.gov.uk/coshh

Houghton Brown, J. (2001) *Horse Business Management*, 3rd edn. Blackwell Science.

Johnson, G. and Scholes, K. (1997) *Exploring Corporate Strategy*, 4th edn. Prentice Hall.

Kotler, P. and Armstrong, G. (2001) *Principles of Marketing*, 9th edn. Prentice Hall.

Kotler, P. (2002) *Marketing Management*, 11th edn. Prentice Hall.

Laurie, D. (2001) *From Battlefield to Boardroom*. Palgrave.

Lipsey, R.G. and Chrystal, K.A. (1999) *Principles of Economics*. Oxford University Press

Lockhart, J. & Wiseman, A.J.L. (1993) *Crop Husbandry including Grassland*, 7th edn. Pergamon Press.

Lynch, R. (2000) *Corporate Strategy*, 2nd edn. Pearson Education.

Maslow, A., cited in Johns, A.E. (1973) *The Sociology of Organisational Change.* Pergamon Press.

Mercer, D. (1996) *Marketing*, 2nd edn. Blackwell Business.

McCormick, S. (2001) *Strategy in Action.* Blackwell Publishing.

Mintzberg, H., Ahlstrand, B., and Lampel, J. (1998) *Strategy Safari.* Prentice Hall.

Nellis, J.G. and Parker, D. (2002) *Principles of Economics.* Pearson Education.

National Office of Animal Health (NOAH) (2001) *Animal Welfare Report Heralds Regulatory Reform.* www.noah.co.uk/pressrel/2001/010510a.htm

Pearsall, J. (1998) *New Oxford Dictionary of English.* Oxford University Press.

Porter, M.E. (1980) *Competitive Strategy.* The Free Press.

Roberts, A. (2002) *Napoleon and Wellington.* Phoenix Press.

Rogers, W. (2001) Cited in McCormick, S. *Strategy in Action.* Blackwell Publishing.

Rumelt, R.P. (1998) Cited in Mintzberg, H., Ahlstrand, B., and Lampel, J. *Strategy Safari.* Prentice Hall.

Tzu, S. (1963) *The Art of War.* Oxford University Press.

Tolkein, J.R.R. (1985) *Lord of the Rings.* Harper Collins.

Further reading

Blanchard, K. and Bowles, S. (1998) *Gung Ho! Motivate the People in any Organisation.* Harper Collins.

Bonoma, T. (1985) Case research in marketing opportunities: problems and a process. *Journal of Marketing Research* **XXII**, 199–208.

Boje, D.M. (2001) *Narrative Methods for Organisational and Communication Research.* Sage Publications.

Boyett, J.H. and Boyett, J.T. (1998) *The Guru Guide.* John Wiley and Sons, Inc.

Burns, A.C. and Bush, R.F. (1998) *Marketing Research*, 2nd edn. Prentice Hall.

Carnall, C.A. (1999) *Managing Change in Organisations.* Prentice Hall.

Carson, D., Gilmore, A., Perry, C. and Gronhaug, K. (2001) *Qualitative Marketing Research.* Sage Publications.

Chopra, D. (1999) *The Seven Spiritual Laws of Success.* Bantam Press.

Cresswell, J.W. (1994) *Research Design – Qualitative and Quantitative Approaches.* Sage Publications.

Curran, J. and Blackburn, R.A. (2001) *Researching the Small Enterprise.* Sage Publications.

Czarniawska, B. (1998) *A Narrative Approach to Organisation Studies.* Sage Publications.

Dawes, F. (1999) *Small Business Management – An Overview.* Blackhall Publishing.

Dunphy, D. and Stace, D.A. (1988) Transformational and coercive strategies for planned organisational change: beyond the organisational development model. *Organisational Studies* **9**(3), 317–34.

Easterby-Smith, M., Thorpe, R. and Lowe, A. (2002) *Management Research: An Introduction*, 2nd edn. Sage Publications.

Eisenhardt, K.M. (1989) Building theories from case study research. *Academy of Management Review* **14**(4), 532–50.

Gibb, A. and Webb, T. (1980) *Policy Issues in Small Business Research*. Saxon House.

Gill, J. and Johnson, P. (1991) *Research Methods for Managers*. Paul Chapman Publishing.

Gluey, J.W. and Maycunich, A. (2000) *Beyond the Learning Organisation*. Perseus Books.

Grundy, M. (2001) Coping with market changes. *In Practice* **23**(3) 174–6.

Gordon, W. (1999) *Good Thinking: A Guide to Qualitative Research*. Admap Publications.

Honey, P. and Mumford, A. (1990) *The Opportunist Learner*. Peter Honey Publications.

Houlden, B. (1996) *Understanding Corporate Strategy: An Introduction*, 2nd edn. Blackwell Publishing.

Hussey, J. and Hussey, R. (1997) *Business Research: A Practical Guide*. Macmillan Business.

Kolb, D. (1984) *Experiential Learning*. Prentice Hall.

Kolb, D. (1996) The management and learning process. In Starkey, K. *How Organisations Learn*. Thompson Business Press.

Malhotra, N.K. and Birks, D.F. (2000) *Marketing Research: An Applied Approach*. Pearson.

Peat Marwick McLintock for the British Horse Society (1988) *The Economic Contribution of the British Equine Industry*. British Horse Society.

Peppard, J. and Rowland, P. (1995) *The Essence of Business Re-Engineering*. Prentice Hall.

Peters, T. and Waterman, R. (1982) *In Search of Excellence*. Harper Collins.

Pettinger, R. (2000) *Mastering Organisational Behaviour*. Macmillan Master Series.

Saunders, M., Lewis, P. and Thornhill, A. (2000) *Research Methods for Business Students*, 2nd edn. Prentice Hall.

Schoemer, K.G. (1998) *The New Reality: How to Make Change your Competitive Advantage*. Penguin Books.

Williams, A.L. (1988) *All You Can Do is All You Can Do*. Ballantine Books.

Index